Cambridge Elements ≡

Elements in the Global Middle Ages
edited by
Geraldine Heng
University of Texas at Austin
Susan J. Noakes
University of Minnesota–Twin Cities

SWAHILI WORLDS IN GLOBALISM

Chapurukha M. Kusimba
University of South Florida

CAMBRIDGE
UNIVERSITY PRESS

Shaftesbury Road, Cambridge CB2 8EA, United Kingdom

One Liberty Plaza, 20th Floor, New York, NY 10006, USA

477 Williamstown Road, Port Melbourne, VIC 3207, Australia

314–321, 3rd Floor, Plot 3, Splendor Forum, Jasola District Centre,
New Delhi – 110025, India

103 Penang Road, #05–06/07, Visioncrest Commercial, Singapore 238467

Cambridge University Press is part of Cambridge University Press & Assessment,
a department of the University of Cambridge.

We share the University's mission to contribute to society through the pursuit of
education, learning and research at the highest international levels of excellence.

www.cambridge.org
Information on this title: www.cambridge.org/9781009495080

DOI: 10.1017/9781009072922

First published 2024

A catalogue record for this publication is available from the British Library

ISBN 978-1-009-49508-0 Hardback
ISBN 978-1-009-07405-6 Paperback
ISSN 2632-3427 (online)
ISSN 2632-3419 (print)

Cambridge University Press & Assessment has no responsibility for the persistence
or accuracy of URLs for external or third-party internet websites referred to in this
publication and does not guarantee that any content on such websites is, or will
remain, accurate or appropriate.

Swahili Worlds in Globalism

Elements in the Global Middle Ages

DOI: 10.1017/9781009072922
First published online: January 2024

Chapurukha M. Kusimba
University of South Florida

Author for correspondence: Chapurukha M. Kusimba, ckusimba@usf.edu

Abstract: This Element discusses a medieval African urban society as a product of interactions among African communities who inhabited the region between 100 BCE and 500 CE. It deviates from standard approaches that credit urbanism and the state in Africa to non-African agents. East Africa, then and now, was part of the broader world of the Indian Ocean. Globalism coincided with the political and economic transformations that occurred during the Tang-Sung-Yuan-Ming dynasties and Islamic times, 600–1500 CE. Positioned as the gateway into and out of eastern Africa, the Swahili coast became a site through which people, inventions, and innovations bidirectionally migrated, were adopted, and evolved. Swahili people's agency and unique characteristics cannot be seen only through Islam's prism. Instead, their unique character is a consequence of social and economic interactions of actors along the coast, inland, and beyond the Indian Ocean.

Keywords: urbanism, globalism, medieval, Swahili, Indian Ocean

ISBNs: 9781009495080 (HB), 9781009074056 (PB), 9781009072922 (OC)
ISSNs: 2632-3427 (online), 2632-3419 (print)

Contents

Introduction: Swahili Worlds – A Medieval African Urban Civilization

Most African nation-states attained political independence from European colonizers and began the slow process of emancipation. The few books they inherited from the colonial governments painted an image of an unchanging Africa awakened from its deep slumber by European missionaries and colonists who saved Africans' souls and gradually guided them to "salvation" and "civilization."

The East African coast, a region where my life and career would later become entangled, was different. Yes, it was in Africa, but we were taught that life on the coast was unlike that of inland Africa. Its culture and civilization were those of Muslim invaders who colonized the region and enslaved millions from inland Africa. These disruptions to African lives were stopped thanks to the work of European antislavery activists and missionaries who risked their lives at sea and in the far inland reaches of Africa to end slavery – the Arab scourge. These teachings are still part of the memory of many East Africans and adversely influence present-day interactions of resources distribution and sharing in modern East Africa. Our textbooks had colorful images of caravans led by ferocious, bearded, whip-wielding men leading chained gangs of emaciated men and women bearing whole ivory tusks to the coast. The teaching was clear: blame Muslims and Arabs for the predicament of Africans.

My first visit to the coast was in 1984 when, as a history student at Kenyatta, I went on a tour of the coast's historical and archeological heritage sites. A second trip followed in 1985, this time with a Swahili language group. These trips impressed me with the richness of coastal history while also exposing the colonial misinformation campaigns. Gedi's majestic ruins, the vibrancy of Swahili poetry, and the rich history of resistance against Portuguese, Omani, German, and British colonization by coastal peoples emerged in stark contrast to notions of a static African past. Historians and archaeologists were challenging these perspectives (Walz, 2013). Historian James de Vere Allen, who began serving as the first curator of the Lamu Museum in 1974, argued that Swahili culture in the Lamu Archipelago of Kenya had revived during the eighteenth and nineteenth centuries despite a drastic decline in maritime trade. Towns succeeded through cooperation with their immediate hinterlands. "[I]t is hard to believe," he emphasized, "the same was not true of earlier periods" (Allen, 1974:138). He elaborated:

> [Trade items] are unlikely to have been brought from the coast without some simultaneous spread of Swahili language and ideas. Iron-working and jewelry styles are among other things that need further investigation before we can deny coast-interior links with any certainty. Nor need it be assumed that unglazed pottery styles and techniques, iron-smelting, and jewelry fashions

must necessarily have spread from the coast to the interior, rather than vice
versa. The very word "Swahili" derives from the Arabic Sahil denoting, in
maritime usage, a port serving as an entrepot for its hinterland's goods. (135)

In his dissertation, which was later published as a monograph, Mark Horton
(1984:235–248, 1996:378–406) posited a more specific link between pastoral
communities in the interior and early coastal populations, through which hinterland items reached Indian Ocean traders. He wrote, "It is more likely [that]
coastal societies obtained their pottery from an inland source as they do today,
and subsequently traded it along the coast. This pottery could have come from
the Tana, Sabaki, or the Usambara hills" (Horton, 1984:296–297). Although
they disagreed, both the historian (Vere Allen) and the archaeologist (Horton)
drew from contemporary analogies to propose and test alternative interpretations of the idea of a seaward-oriented Swahili and a coast-hinterland dichot-
omy in the region.

Understanding a culture, especially one like that of the medieval Swahili of
East Africa, requires unscrambling half a millennium of colonization: conquest
by the Portuguese in the late fifteenth century, rule by the Omani Arabs who
followed in the eighteenth century, and occupation by Britain and Germany
after the Berlin Conference of 1884 partitioned Africa. Colonization led to an
influx of immigrants. Some stayed temporarily; others intermingled with locals.
Many made money and returned to their homelands. The medieval towns of the
East African coast were inhabited by people from the diverse places with which
these towns interacted.

In the recent history of the East African coast, members of the elite, no longer
in power, conspired against one another, allying with colonizers in numerous
ways, including intermarriage. Climate change and conquest led to large-scale
abandonment, migration, and flight to safer regions. The institutionalization of
slavery in the eighteenth and nineteenth centuries revealed the trauma of
coexistence. These experiences present us with the ominous task of writing
a history informed largely by an archaeological landscape of only standing
ruined architecture and colonial descendants' accounts. This Element repre-
sents my humble attempt to unscramble aspects of the experience of the proud
people who gave East and Central Africans a language to unite them.

1 Foundations of a Medieval African Urban Civilization

What was it like to build and sustain community life and to interact with one's
neighbors in the sixth through fifteenth centuries CE in coastal Africa? What
resources existed, and how were they used to build and maintain communities?
This Element examines factors crucial to a state society's rise and sustenance in

a region dominated by non-state societies (e.g., Stanish, 2017). Its core questions are: How did leadership emerge, sustain itself, and transform society? Why and how did social inequalities evolve, persist, and diminish, and with what consequences? How did market systems emerge, continue, and change? How did the organization of Swahili communities at varying scales emerge from and constrain their members' actions? What evidence is there for the relationships medieval Swahili forged with their inland and coastal neighbors and Indian Ocean partners?

This Element is part of a larger effort initiated by Geraldine Heng and Susan Noakes to understand the Global Middle Ages and the interconnections that preceded the new globalization. Through a series of advanced seminars, workshops, and conferences, the Global Middle Ages Consortium – the East African component of which I directed – of scholars drawn from the humanities and social sciences has collected a huge database that is unraveling the everyday experiences of previously anonymous human communities who engaged in early global interactions.[1] The emerging picture reveals complex extra-regional interaction spheres that connected people, enabling the multi-directional migrations of people and ideas, and the circulation of resources. These interactions shaped the course of history and in many ways preceded later forms of unequal relationships that characterize global relationships today.

The foundations of coastal urban society are owed to interactions among foraging, fishing, pastoral, and agricultural communities who inhabited the coast between 100 BCE and 500 CE (Mathew, 1956:65). The urban polities that emerged in this region during the medieval period were politically autonomous, oligarchic, matrilineal, and mercantile in character (Chami, 1998; Horton and Chami, 2018; Middleton, 1992:100; Figure 1). Like in many regions in the broader world of the Indian Ocean, the emergence of globalization coincided with the sociopolitical and economic transformations that occurred during the Tang-Sung-Yuan-Ming and Islamic dynastic times, 600–1500 CE (Beaujard, 2019; Kusimba, 2017). Steward Gordon (2009) refers to this as the era "when Asia was the world." The East African coast was the gateway into and out of eastern Africa for Asians and the rest of the world. Today, the Swahili language is spoken from Mombasa in East Africa to Kinshasa in Central Africa, affirming the interregional connectivity (Fabian, 1991). Coastal residents, both urban and rural, have embraced Islam as their religion, but both the African and Muslim ethos play significant roles in their daily lives.

---

[1] http://globalmiddleages.org/project/early-global-connections-east-africa-between-asia-and-medi terranean-europe.

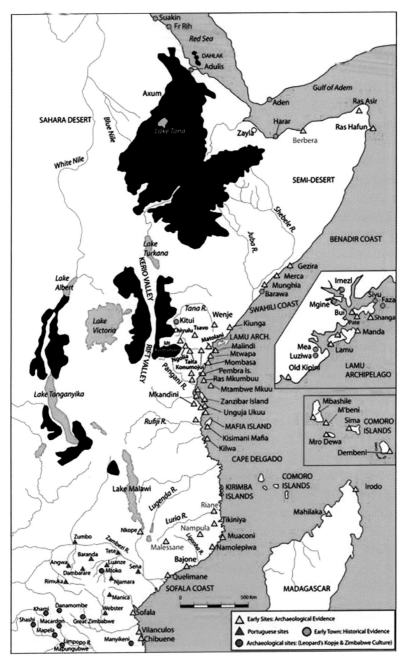

Figure 1 Map of eastern and southern Africa showing known towns that engaged in global trade (Credit: Foreman Bandama, the Field Museum, Chicago, IL, USA)

The Swahili people's agency and unique characteristics cannot be singularly seen through Islam's prism (Becker, 2018). State societies display a recognizable group of diagnostic features, including urbanism, ethnic diversity, social stratification, political organization, specialization, and long-distance exchange. While each state has its unique history, each rose through the combined action of the same small set of factors (Carneiro, 2012:6).

The East African coast was one of the bridges over which early Africans left the continent to form a diaspora inhabiting the rest of the world. Since the Bronze Age, East Africa has served as one of the major gateways through which people, ideas, domesticated plants and animals, and other innovations reached or left Africa (Boivin et al., 2014; Fuller et al., 2011; Rowlands and Fuller, 2018). Located on the western edge of the pan-Indian Ocean, the Swahili coast shares all the contemporary cultural accouterments of the wider Indian Ocean world: an expanse of trade networks, religious persuasions, cuisine, and fashion (Walshaw, 2015). This Element highlights how towns, cities, villages, and hinterlands along the coastline adjusted to integrate into the global networks of the medieval period.

The Politics of Identity and Invention of History

Today the multiple ethnic groups who have collaborated in shaping the coastal region's landscape and cultural history over the past two millennia belong to two dominant language groups: Bantu and Cushite (Table 1). In coastal Kenya, for example, the Bantu speakers referred to as the northeast coast Sabaki subfamily include the Swahili, Mijikenda, Pokomo, and Malakote (Nurse and Spear, 1985). The Cushite speakers include the Somali, Oromo, and several foraging communities (Stiles, 1981). The founding and sustenance of the medieval towns and polities of the East African coast must be credited to the contributions of these groups. Coastal urbanism arose in locales inhabited predominantly by people who spoke Kingozi, which later became popularly known as Swahili. As Swahili is one of the few written precolonial languages in East Africa and widely adopted as a lingua franca, its dominance and popularity in East and Central Africa are unmatched. Today it is one of the most widely spoken languages in East and Central Africa (Fabian, 1991).

Swahili culture is as much a consequence of geography as it is of human agency. The coast's unique location on the western end of the Indian Ocean made it a natural gateway and point of exit for people, ideas, goods, and services. The coastal peoples have interacted with partners in inland East Africa, the Persian and Arabian Gulfs, the Indian subcontinent, and Indonesia for much of the past three millennia (Beaujard, 2018). During this period, a multitude of items in high demand across Europe, Asia, and Africa were

Table 1 Communities of the East African coast

Coast	Ecological zone	Community
Benadir coast	seashore	Swahili, Bantu of the Shabelle and Jubba valleys, Somali
	hinterland	Somali, Orma
northern coast	lowland forest	Boni, Dahalo, Waata
	dry rangelands	Orma and Somali
	river valleys	Pokomo and Elwana
	islands	Swahili
Nyali coast	Nyika	Segeju, Mijikenda
	seashore	Segeju, Mijikenda
	islands	Swahili
Mrima coast	Nyika	Kwere, Shambaa, Zaramo, Zigula, Doe
	seashore	Bondei, Doe, Mijikenda Segeju, Swahili, Zaramo,
	islands	Swahili
Mgao coast	Nyika	Makonde, Ndengereko, Ngindo, Yao
	islands	Swahili
Kerimba coast		Mwani
Comoros	islands	Maore, Ngazidja, Ndzuwani Mwali

exchanged, ranging from spices, ivory, frankincense, myrrh, silks, sandalwood, and other exotica to grains, cattle, metal ores, goods, and other commodities (Oka, 2018:334). These trade pursuits simultaneously created great wealth and inequities.

Medieval East African coastal urban society was maritime with a subsistence economy centered on fishing, farming, craft production, and trade (Sarathi, 2015). The market economy was based on mixed farming and cereal agriculture, as well as millet, sorghum, and rice farming. People kept cattle, goats, and donkeys. Mangrove poles, dried fish, skins, hides, cereals, ivory, and rhinoceros horn formed the bulk of significant exports (Table 2). Social and economic disparities are reflected in the spatial organization of these medieval settlements. Islam was introduced in the ninth century, and by the end of the medieval period, it had become the dominant religion. Many anonymous individuals from diverse social and cultural backgrounds, both Muslim and non-Muslim, lived side by side in the East African coast's medieval settlements. Reconstructing these medieval experiences is the task of this Element.

Table 2 Coastal ecological zones, rainfall distributions, and subsistence economy

Ecological zone	Annual rainfall	People	Subsistence
Northern Somalia (Guban)	80 mm	Somali	pastoralists, foragers
Oogo mountain range	500–750 mm	Somali	pastoralists, foragers
Nugal valley	400–500 mm	Somali	pastoralists, foragers
Hawd plateau	250–300 mm	Somali	pastoralists, foragers
Shabelle and Juba river valleys		Ribi and Boni, Reer Shabeelle, Gosha, Hawiye, Raxanweyn	farmers, fishers, pastoralists, foragers
Southern Somalia (Banaadir and Kismaayo regions)		Eyle, Somali	farmers, fishers, sailors, artisans
Lamu Archipelago	1,000 mm	Boni (Aweera) Orma, Swahili	foragers, farmers, fishers, pastoralists, sailors, artisans
Tana delta	800–1,200 mm	Pokomo, Malakote, Swahili, Dahalo	farmers, fishers, sailors, artisans
Nyali coast	1,000 mm	Mijikenda, Swahili, Waata	farmers, fishers, sailors, artisans
Nyali hinterland	800–1,200 mm	Mijikenda, Waata, Orma, Wakyankuru	pastoralists, farmers, foragers
Interior		Kamba, Orma, Taita, Walyankuru	farmers, pastoralists, foragers, hunters
Mrima coast	1,000 mm	Swahili, Mijikenda, Seutu	farmers, fishers, artisans
Mrima hinterland	800–1,200 mm	Kutu, Kwere, Doa	farmers
Zanzibar	1,400 mm	Swahili	farmers, fishers, artisans
Pemba	2,000 mm	Swahili	farmers, fishers, artisans

Swahili is a Bantu language and Arabic is a Semitic language. Because of centuries of interaction and conversion to Islam, standard Swahili has borrowed words from Arabic that reflect cultural values, religious-moral values, and literature (Mkilifi, 1972:197). The influence of Arabic on Swahili is illustrated in a popular couplet attributed to elite Swahili during the colonial period:

> *Kiswahili halawa, lugha yake sawa sawa*
> *Mdai bingwa hajawa, Kiarabu kutofahama.*
> Kiswahili is sweetness, it is a sound
> language but no one can claim he is an
> expert of it if he does not understand Arabic.
> (Salim, 1985:224)

The historical and political context of this couplet points to the broad question of identity. Social distancing from things African, which, at the time, connoted inferiority, contributed to the invention of ancestry traditions that credited a medieval Swahili founding to foreign diaspora immigrants from the Muslim world in the Persian Gulf (Ray, 2003). As part of the wider Muslim world, elite African families sent their children to be educated in Muslim universities such as al-Azhar University in Egypt. Nineteenth-century elite Swahili households were bilingual. Arabic, Hindi, Persian, and Urdu were often spoken in the homes of a growing Omani and Yemeni diaspora. Fluency in Arabic and Kingozi (classical Swahili) were crucial for understanding Swahili poetry and other historical renderings. Then the elite read widely and understood multiple languages through which they interacted as members of the Indian Ocean trading diaspora. Sayyid Abdalla bin Ali bin Nassir's epic *Al Inkishafi* (*Catechism of a Soul*) lamenting the decline of Pate, written circa 1800 CE, captures the intertwined histories of Islamic culture and art in the Swahili cultural system:

> *BISMILLAHI naiqadimu*
> *hali ya kutuga hino nudhumu*
> *na AR-RAHMANI kirasimu*
> *basi AR-RAHIMI nyumba ikaye*
>
> *Nataka himdi nitangulize*
> *ili mdadisi asiulize*
> *akamba himdi uitusilize*
> *kapakaza illa isiyo nduye*
>
> *Ikisa himdi kutabalaji*
> *ikizagaa kama siraji*
> *sala and salamu kiidariji*
> *tumwa Muhammmadi nimsaliye*
> *Na alize thama banu Kinana*
> *na Sahaba wane wenyi maina*

tusalie wote ajmaina
sala and mbawazi ziwaaliye

Let us first invoke the Mighty Name of God: Allah Ar-Rahman
Ar Rahim God merciful, God Benign!
Thus, let us open, that none be denied
The virtue to be gained from saying His Name
Nor do the critics blame us for omitting it
That were, indeed, a sin unparalleled.

Once made, this invocation is a lamp
To light our way: next follow prayers and Peace.
For our prophet Mohammad, let us pray

And his kinsfolk of the Qinan tribe
And for the four companions of the Name:
For all of them we pray and ask God's peace,
May our prayers and fealty sustain them all.
(Allen, 1977:25, 51)

Medieval East Africa, to which the Swahili belonged, was a complex world –
a product of dynamic interactions of coastal peoples – occupying a central
position geographically and culturally, with both other African and non-African
cultures. Its history cannot be understood solely through one lens or the other, be
it Islamic or African, coastal or hinterland, foreign or local (Kusimba et al.,
1994:51). This Element narrates how this dynamic and resilient African civilization came into being and how it sustained itself.

2 The Rise of the Medieval Swahili State

Introduction

In this section, we discuss the factors that contributed to the rise of state
societies in eastern and southern Africa, the regional connections that these
African states developed and maintained, and the consequences of cooperation
between the regions for the state's sustenance. We show that without these
earlier regional relationships, the wealth exhibited in the East African coast's
medieval cities would have taken on a different trajectory.

The Rise of the Medieval Swahili State

Between 800 and 1500 CE, towns and city-states arose on the East African
coast, replacing non-state societies that had existed in the region during the
Early Iron Age (ca. 500 BCE–500 CE). These transformations from non-state to
state societies were regional in scope and have been tied to the restoration of
stability in the Indian Ocean and the Persian Gulf following the rise of Islam.
Early and Late Iron Age non-state societies in East Africa interacted through

Table 3 Major food crops grown in Africa

Indigenous	*Non Indigenous*
yams, pearl/bullrush millet, cowpea, guinea millet, gourd, sesame (West Africa)	maize (New World)
African rice (*Oryza glaberrima*)	cassava (New World)
sorghum (numerous kinds), fonio, African rice, legumes such as pigeon peas, garden greens (Sahel, Ethiopia)	wheat (Southwest Asia)
finger millet (East Africa)	bananas (Southeast Asia)
	flax (Southwest Asia)
Teff, Ensete coffee, Noog (Ethiopia)	

regional trade networks (Kusimba, 1999:2). However, during the medieval period, there was expansion in trade and interaction to include the wider Indian Ocean, Persian Gulf, and regions beyond, as far as East Asia.

The medieval landscape of East Africa reveals the richness and diversity of connections with the African interior that provide new ways of viewing the global economic, social, and political order between 800 and 1500 CE that became dominated by the Silk Road commercial complex (Broadman, 2007; Comas et al., 1998; Elverskog, 2011). For example, the food served today across the region tells the triumphant story of these interactions, connections, and contributions. Contributions from archaeobotany, which were long absent in the interpretation of relationships, are beginning to provide an excellent prism through which to view the interactions in the Afrasian world (Fuller et al., 2011; Rowlands and Fuller, 2018; Table 3). It is unlikely that the full list of exchanged goods and the precise time they crossed the seas out of or into Africa will ever be known. What we do know is that human agency was a prime mover of agricultural innovation, and these early attempts to move domesticated animals and plants were complex endeavors that point to the nature, scope, and intensity of first connections and interaction spheres.

The Chronological Context of Medieval African Society

Accurate determination of the time at which past events occurred is the cornerstone of archaeology because without this, interpreting the material evidence becomes deeply flawed and problematic. The use of other dating methods – for example, relative dating – is not only because the radiocarbon method is expensive but because relative dating is sometimes more accurate and refined and provides tighter chronologies. In this Element, I use five broad periods to discuss the evolutionary process of urbanism, illustrated in Table 4. I briefly discuss each period and its associated sites along with general implications.

Table 4 Periodization of coastal and inland archaeology

Stages of development	Associations	Associated sites	Estimated population per settlement
First stage (100 BCE–700 CE)	Early farming and herding communities in dispersed villages, no evidence of social differentiation and ranking	Unguja Ukuu, Ras Hafun, Kwale, Manda, Kilwa, KiMa1, KiMa9, Misasa, Mpiji, Kiwangwa, Masuguru, Chibuene	< 500
Second stage (700–800 CE)	The elaboration of interregional trade and introduction of external trade	Pemba, Tumbe, Shanga, Ungwana, Kaole, Zhizo, Changwehela	500–1,000
Third stage (800–1000 CE)	Increase in volume and scale of trade, the emergence of chiefdoms, cooperation in building elite and ritual residences, evidence of social ranking	Kima6, Kirongwe, Lamu, Mombasa, Malindi, Kilifi	2,000–5,000
Fourth stage (1000–1500 CE)	The state emerges, characterized by dry stone in inland southern Africa and coral rag architecture along the coast	Mapungubwe, Mapela, K2, Great Zimbabwe, Leopard Kopje, Gumanye, Mtwapa, Manda, Shanga, Pemba, Kilwa	5,000–20,000
Fifth stage (1500–1900 CE)	European contact and rise of transatlantic slave trade, conquest, and colonization	Mutapa, European and Oman fortresses	Variable

The Early Iron Age (500 BCE–500 CE)

The African Early Iron Age, dated between 500 BCE and 500 CE, refers to non-state iron-using societies that inhabited eastern, Central, and southern Africa (Chami, 1999; Phillipson, 1977). Historical linguists associate coastal settlements from this period with Proto-Sabaki Bantu and pastoral Cushitic speakers (Ehret and Nurse, 1981; Nurse, 1983). Settlements were small and most were inhabited seasonally by seminomadic hunter-gatherers and fisher-folk. Archaeological remains from these settlements indicate that the inhabitants had a basic knowledge of gardening and engaged in barter with their neighbors. Their pottery, known as Kwale ware, had beveled, fluted rims and shoulders. A small percentage of these wares were decorated with narrow, incised, and stamped bands. They were open-fired and designed to be used to prepare stewed food (Chittick, 1969:122; Phillipson, 1977:109–110; Pouwels, 1987:10; Soper, 1971).

Few Iron Age settlements have been intensively studied on the East African coast (Soper, 1971). Evidence of food production and gathering, iron metallurgy, pottery making and use, cow farming, fishing, and hunting has been recovered at these sites. Exchange networks among the agricultural, pastoral, and foraging communities have not been conclusively ascertained but were highly probable and involved reciprocal relations that were also embedded in feasting and other communal activities (Harris, 1965:182).

The archaeological record shows early coastal inhabitants as farmers, fishers, and ironworkers who settled on the coast in the later centuries BCE. These communities preferred to settle in areas with permanent water, including river mouths, creeks, and deltas. To supplement inaccessible resources, they used dug-out canoes, *mtumbwi*, to sail up rivers and streams and along the coast to fish and barter with their pastoralist and forager neighbors. The early farming inhabitants of the coast spoke Proto-Sabaki Bantu and Proto-Cushitic languages. Historical linguists have proposed that the Proto-Sabaki emerged as a distinct linguistic group north of the Ruvu River region in northeastern Tanzania around the middle of the first millennium CE or soon after that (Ehret and Nurse, 1981; Nurse and Hinnesbusch, 1993). Proto-Sabaki spread northward along the coast into the hinterland, occupying much of their present occupation and incorporating earlier inhabitants into their society. They were principally cultivators and keepers of sheep and goats and some cattle (Helm, et al., 2012; Mutoro, 1987:25).

Settling along shallow beaches with minimal harbor facilities resonates with a deliberate choice to exploit food resources available in the coral reefs, inlets, bays, creeks, and mangrove swamps. Cereals such as millet, sorghum, and sesame, as well as coconuts and fruit trees, were farmed in the fertile, well-watered soils of offshore islands. Open spaces cleared for shifting agriculture became grazing land for livestock. Wild game was hunted for meat and hides.

Ethnic affiliations and cultural identities develop from peoples' interaction with their environment. Their awareness as a distinct cultural group is profoundly affected by their collective experiences of the world they live in, both in time and in space. Commenting on Stage I coastal inhabitants, historian Randall Pouwels (1987:23) wrote:

> Bantu groups mainly had a relatively sophisticated technological and intellectual tradition adapted to exploit the full range of coastal resources. But the sea presented additional opportunities. The marine technology they developed out of (apparently) rudimentary fishing and canoe-making skills they had inherited from their continental ancestors, however, represented a real innovation meant to take advantage of a part of this environment in which their forefathers and cousins did not have. Coastal Africans actively and consciously innovated and adjusted to pursue new possibilities.

The Late Iron Age (500–800 CE)

Most settlements from the Early Iron Age survived into the Late Iron Age. They include sites like Gezira, Irodo, Kaole, Kilwa, Mahilaka, Manda, Monapo, Pate, and Shanga. Large quantities of local pottery, iron artifacts, and ostrich and marine shell beads dominate the archaeological finds (Wynne-Jones, 2014:53). Nonlocal artifacts, such as trade ceramics, glass, and glass beads, appear during this time. Continuity in local stylistic traditions is indicated by the fact that more than 40 percent of decorative motifs seen in the previous stage continued to be used. A new type of decorative motif characterized by triangular, oblique, and double zig-zag incisions was introduced, which is known as Triangular-Incised or Tana ware (Chami, 1994:13; Horton, 1996:243). This pottery was used across much of eastern Africa from the coast into the far reaches of western Tanzania (Ichumbaki and Pollard 2015; Mapunda, 1995; Figure 2).

The settlement size increased from one to two hectares during the Iron Age. The estimated average population ranged from 500 to 2,000 persons at the largest settlements. Houses remained circular, spherical, and cylindrical. Based on the large finds, archaeologists determined these settlements were occupied permanently as sedentary villages (LaViolette and Fleisher, 2005). Residents hunted, fished, gathered, farmed, and bartered with their neighbors and carried out local and interregional trade. The greater diversity in pottery styles,

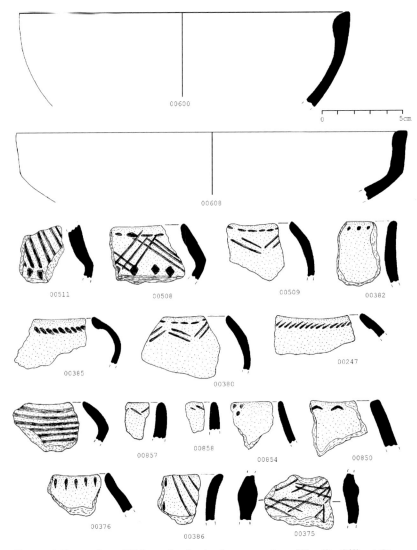

Figure 2 Examples of Triangular-Incised ware pottery (Credit: Gilbert Oteyo, British Institute of Eastern Africa, Nairobi)

especially the appearance of non-African trade items, provides evidence for the beginning of maritime trade on a limited scale.

The Early Medieval Period (800–1250 CE)

The early medieval period saw a rise in investment in crafts specialization beyond the household. This is seen in the installation of iron smelting workshops in the rural areas and blacksmithing in the more urban and densely inhabited

Figure 3 Micrograph of crucible steel from Galu (Credit: Chapurukha
M. Kusimba, University of South Florida)

settlements. So lucrative was the iron industry that some settlements appear to
have grown to specialize in iron processing. One such center was Gedi on the
Nyali coast, where Kirkman (1956:23) reports large quantities of iron-stone
pebbles and slag. This led him to propose that Gedi was one of the ironworking
centers of Malindi described by the Arab geographers such as Al Masudi, Al
Idrisi, and Al Biruni (Freeman-Grenville, 1962:20). The coastal ironworkers were
investing in iron production for both local and regional demand, including the
making and selling of crucible steel (Kusimba et al., 1994, Figure 3).

Many other activities were by-products of investment in ironworking, including diving for pearls, mining amber, and hunting specifically for ivory, leopard
skins, and turtles. Interregional trade into inland Africa was organized to secure
gold and copper, which at this time were in high demand in the Persian Gulf
(Verin, 1986:57).

The Late Medieval Period (1250–1500 CE)

The majority of settlements founded in the early medieval period developed into
towns and city-states. Some city-states, including Mogadishu, Pate, Lamu,
Ungwana, Malindi, Mombasa, Kilwa, and Mahilaka, became major cosmopolitan
centers that attracted merchants, artisans, artists, craftspeople, and unskilled
workers across the broader region for work and commerce (LaViolette, 2008).
Intensive agricultural investment was developed in the hinterlands to support the
burgeoning urban populations (Kusimba and Kusimba, 2018; Walz, 2009). The
estimated population size at these medieval settlements ranged from 5,000 to as
many as 20,000 residents. The population of the more rural settlements remained
small as migration to more established city-states increased.

The standardized placement of streets and residential homes in a less hap-hazard manner reveals urban planning, and self-contained homes equipped with toilets (pit latrines), internal plumbing, and baths at Gedi, Manda, Mtwapa, Ungwana, and Shanga testify to the prosperity of the elite. The first coral-walled buildings indicate a rise in wealthy families that could afford to build and maintain stone houses. Cut coral, called porites, was used for doorjambs, mosque mihrabs, and decoration in elite homes. Moreover, mortuary and funerary behavioral changes are seen in the widespread use of paneled and pillar tombs from Somalia to Madagascar (Allen and Wilson, 1979). Pillar tombs replaced the earlier domed ones found at Kilwa and Mahilaka (Kirkman, 1957:18; Verin, 1986:60). Settlement patterns also changed dramat-ically. Neighborhoods segregated by minor walls symbolized kinship, social, economic, and religious affiliations.

Excavations of domestic architecture at Kilwa Kisiwani, Gedi, Ungwana, Manda, Shanga, and Mtwapa suggest that fourteenth-century house plans included a more expansive sunken courtyard, a *baraza* or *kiwanda*, a platform in front of the façade of the house, a long room with a washroom at one end, and two other long rooms separated into four by a corridor. One of the long rooms at Mtwapa, for example, was a storeroom for valuables with a trapdoor near the roof. Some wealthier houses had a walled courtyard behind the house (Kirkman 1966:347). Most activities were carried out in the *kiwanda*, particularly cook-ing, following the old practice of cooking outside the house. Clothes and other household belongings were cleaned in the courtyard. Living room floors were made with gravel and finished with lime. The installation in elite homes of pit latrines with a wash bench with bidets for the ablution pot occurred at this time (Kirkman, 1957:22).

As towns' populations expanded, empty spaces were filled in with new homes, but some of the wealthier residents appear to have retained larger areas around their homes for use as gardens and corrals for cattle. This is the first critical evidence for apparent socioeconomic and class differences. The upper class of these towns and cities monopolized wealth-creating resources, including the labor of commoners whom Hans Mayr reported as enslaved (Chittick, 1974:249).

The large volume of archaeological remains recovered at these settlements, including iron slag, local earthenware pottery, fish bones, shells, and terrestrial fauna, indicates increased production to satisfy both local and nonlocal demand. Increased debris is also consistent with beyond natural population growth. Population growth is attributed to immigration by coastal, hinterland, and Southwest and South Asian merchants who sought to benefit from the booming economy of emerging medieval African cities like Kilwa, Manda, Mogadishu,

Gedi, and Sofala. The dominance of South Asian merchants is visible at this time and throughout the medieval period as they would play a dominant role as creditors, financiers, and shipwrights (Oka, 2018).

Despite Islam's relatively early introduction into East Africa in the ninth century, conversion to Islam began in earnest during the latter phase of the medieval period, especially in the fourteenth and fifteenth centuries. The first mosque at Shanga dates to the ninth century and mosques would become common on the coast around the mid-fourteenth century (Horton 1996, 2004). Mosques were initially small but gradually increased in size as more people converted to Islam. Investments in stone-built mosques point to Islam's growing popularity and acceptance.

By the fourteenth century, the mosque had become the most imposing building in most coastal settlements. It was made of the most durable materials, such as cut coral and porites coral. Despite Islam's acceptance by the local populations, not everyone converted during the medieval period (Kusimba and Walz, 2018). When Moroccan globetrotter Ibn Batuta visited Kilwa in 1331, he found the town's inhabitants "engaged in a holy war, for their country lies beside that of Pagan Zanj" (Freeman-Grenville, 1962:31).

The general plan for mosques consisted of a *musalla*, a rectangular structure, with a *mihrab*, niches at the north end facing the holy cities of Mecca and Medina. Depending on their size, mosques had anterooms on one or both sides of the *musalla*. A verandah and ablution facilities were located east of the *musalla*. Most Friday mosques of this period were roofed by coral tiles set in lime concrete. The tiles were supported by wooden beams that rested on square or rectangular pillars. Most mosques had one or two rows of pillars (Figure 4).

The west end of the mosque was often reserved for tombs. These became more elaborate during the fourteenth and fifteenth centuries, including circular, rectangular, or polygonal pillars and paneled façades. These pillars were also decorated with porcelain bowls, Arabic scripts, and Qur'anic citations (Baumanova, 2018; Meier, 2016). Although those interred in these tombs are Muslims, this style of pillar is not common in the Middle East. The coastal pillars may be related to phallic megaliths such as those reported in Harar and Sidamo in Ethiopia (Pouwels, 1987:27; Sanseverino, 1983:152). Allen (1981:313) suggested the pillars are identical in structure and function to *vigango*, posts created by the Mijikenda. Pouwels (1987:218) noted the Mijikenda vigango might have come from the coast and not the other way around as no Mijikenda settlements known so far predate those on the coast. Mutoro (1987) has since shown that some Mijikenda settlements date to the tenth century. Pillars on African tombs show that only men are interred.

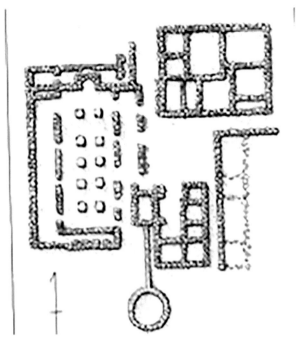

Figure 4 Mosque plan from Mtwapa (Credit: Eric Wert, Field Museum, Chicago, IL, USA)

Women's graves were instead decorated with expensive porcelain that the dead used in life (Figures 5 and 6).

The growing prosperity of East African peoples increased the market for exotica from the African interior as well as the Indian Ocean and the Persian Gulf. Islamic sgraffito pottery, Chinese Qing Bai and Cizhou ware (1200/1250–1400 CE), and chlorite schist from Madagascar and Zimbabwe became the primary ceramics and porcelain used in the homes of wealthy coastal peoples. Bronze mirrors, kohl sticks, glass, and rock crystal beads from the Kenyan interior were part of women's wardrobes. Cooking ovens, *gae la mofa*, and earthenware crucibles are found for the first time, indicating the addition of baking to boiling and roasting cooking styles. Spindle whorls appear at most settlements, signaling increased investment in textile production, particularly the weaving of raffia and tree cotton cloth. Most spindle whorls were recycled local pottery, some were of primary clay sources, and a few were from imported pottery. The Middle Eastern buff-fabric pottery, which is softer than Far Eastern kaolinite wares, was preferred. The appearance of copper and silver coins toward the end of the twelfth century suggests an attempt to unify the region's exchange system and extend and exert political control by the rulers of Kilwa, Manda, and Shanga beyond their city's boundaries. Each city population

Figure 5 Pillar tomb believed to house elite men (Credit: Chapurukha M. Kusimba, University of South Florida)

Figure 6 Domed tomb believed to host elite women (Credit: Chapurukha M. Kusimba, University of South Florida)

appears to have made its own coins, but in general, merchants used coin currency over much of the coast (Perkins et al., 2014).

During the fourteenth century, Chinese celadons, especially Longquan and Tongan (1250–1500 CE), and Sawankhalok or Sisatchanalai jars from Annan or Cambodia (1350–1450/1500 CE) dominated the imported ceramics (Kirkman, 1957:18). Demand for Indian beads and Egyptian glass continued, and sprinkler bottles and bowls in green, white, smoky, and cobalt glass were also in use (Dussubieux et al., 2008). Glass beads in blue, green, and purple were mostly biconical, spherical, barrel, square, or melon in shape. Other beads had white, yellow, or brown strands wound together (Oteyo and Kusimba, 2019). The volume of spindle whorls increased at Kilwa, Pate, and Mogadishu, implying the textile industry's expansion in response to growing regional and possibly international demand. Kilwa and Mogadishu's rulers built copper mints for these cities during the fourteenth century to unify and extend their economic influence beyond their polities (Rothman, 2002).

The diversification of local earthenware is consistent with the increasing economic vitality and cultural diversity of East African coastal material culture. Carinated pots became more common than the large, shouldered bowls, but did not replace them entirely. Medium-necked pots were introduced in the mid-fourteenth century and quickly became standard. Thick, round-bottomed bowls with incised motifs on flat rims (with an average fabric thickness of 6 mm) appeared in the mid-fourteenth century. By 1500, they had almost completely replaced thin-bodied bowls (with an average of 3 mm material thickness). Kirkman (1956:94) excavated a large volume of round-bottomed bowls at Gedi dated to the fourteenth century. The use of red ochre as a burnishing material, previously confined to incurved bowls from earlier contexts at Ungwana, Manda, Shanga, and other sites north of the Tana, now extended to a variety of forms and jars, including the fourteenth-century neckless jars.

The medieval cities of the East African coast reached their pinnacle in the fifteenth century. Settlements that had begun as modest fishing and slash-and-burn hamlets had gradually developed into towns and cities with an economy intimately connected to Indian Ocean commerce (Table 5). The exponential increase in prosperity of the local elite allowed them to purchase more expensive household materials: ceramics, clothes, carnelian beads, perfumes, and rare bronze mirrors sourced from North Africa, the Red Sea, the Persian Gulf, and South and East Asia.

The Effects of Urbanism on Consumption

How did urbanization influence consumption? One way we might assess this is to examine changes in form, function, style, and discard in local earthenware

Table 5 Classification of coastal settlements

Class	Size (hectares)	Features present	Settlement type	Number of sites	Examples of sites
5	1.0	0–1 mosque, < 5 tombs	hamlet	34	Mgangani, Kinuni, Kong, Munje, Diani, Tiwi
4	< 2.5	1–2 mosques, > 5–10 tombs, 1–5 stone houses	village	39	She Umuro, Mwana Mchama, Kilepwa, Mnarani, Shirazi, Rubu, Tumbe, Galu
3	2.5–5.0	1–2 mosques, > 10 stone houses and perimeters walls, > 20 tombs	small town	19	Koyama, Ngumi, Chula, Ishakani, Kiunga, Omwe, Shee Jafari, Kitoka, Jumba la Mtwana. Dondo
2	5.0–15.0	2 mosques, > 2 cemeteries, 50–100 stone houses, enclosed stone houses, mud and stone houses	towns	9	Merka, Munghia, Burgao, Siyu, Shanga, Manda, Mwana, Mtwapa, Vumbu Kuu
1	> 15	> 3 mosques, > 3 cemeteries, > 100 stone houses, estates	cities	8	Mogadishu, Barawa, Malindi, Lamu, Mombasa, Pate, Ungwana, Gede

pottery. Toward the end of the thirteenth century, shouldered bowls and bowls with incised motifs on their rims or sides disappeared from the local markets and were replaced by serving bowls with bases. Innovations in serving bowls point to changes in table etiquette. Food was now served in individual bowls rather than in communal reed baskets. Changes in kitchenware hint at new forms of furniture (perhaps serving tables) and family reorganization to smaller, more nucleated households. At the same time, consumers' tastes might have begun to influence the design and shape of vessels. Those made for urban consumers would have been responsive to the needs of those clients, creating clear distinctions between dishes made for the more rural areas versus those made for the urban market. These distinctions were noted between pottery used at urban Mtwapa and that used at rural Kizingitini, five kilometers inland (Kusimba et al., 2013).

There were also regional differences, but these differences were likely due to local raw material and consumer preferences. For example, pottery vessels made north of the Tana for the residents of Ungwana and Mwana in the Tana Delta continued to be dominated by red-painted burnished ware. At the same time, those south of the Tana at Gedi, Kilepwa, Mtwapa, and Mnarani featured linear-patterned burnished wares. The appearance of any one of these wares north or south of its most common context would imply trade, gift exchange, rural–city migration, or intermarriage.

Medium-necked pots with fingernail impressions replaced the earlier narrow-necked pots. Long-necked cooking pots appeared in the mid-fifteenth century, gradually replacing short-necked pots whose use declined such that by the end of the century, they were scarce in significant towns like Gedi, Kilepwa, Mtwapa. Jars with out-turned necks and incised motifs on the shoulders replaced the earlier jars, which had incised marks on the neck. Fourteenth-century lamps were shallow with rounded sides, while those of the fifteenth century had short vertical sides and pointed ends (Kirkman, 1956:96). Carinated pots were introduced in the early medieval period and continued to be made into contemporary times (Figure 7). The data strongly suggest that these stylistic changes in local pottery signal professionalization of craft technologies in response to demographic changes in the cultural and ethnic makeup of coastal societies.

As the East African coast increasingly became an important trading hub in the wider Indian Ocean and Persian Gulf global networks, its resources provided many attractive economic opportunities. The diversity of consumers spurred potters to modify pots and vessels in response to consumers' tastes. Demand for pottery led to the development of full-time professional potters' guilds, as indicated by the appearance of potters' marks.

Figure 7 Fine examples of modern carinated vessels sold along Mombasa Road

In terms of the trade in ceramics, Chinese Longquan, Tongan, other celadon varieties, and Ying Ch'ing were popular fifteenth-century ceramics (Chittick, 1984:70; Kirkman, 1963:48). Chinese blue-and-white pottery remained popular, but its volume declined in the early part of the fifteenth century. Political rivalry in China led the Chinese government to reject the outside world (1440–1500), resulting in declining ceramic exports. By the late 1480s, the blue-and-white kilns had sufficiently recovered to begin reexporting the popular bowls. By the end of the century, the Chinese blue-and-white porcelain market regained its popularity in the Indian Ocean over celadons (Zhao, 2012; Zhao and Qin, 2018).

Trade with the Persian Gulf rejuvenated in the mid-fifteenth century. Black-on-yellow Islamic pottery, popular in the fourteenth century was replaced by glossy monochromes of blue, green, purple, lavender, grey-slate, brown, yellow, black, and white glazes. The most common Islamic ware were dishes with flat lips and bowls with rounded sides. This is in contrast to the black-and-yellow ware of the thirteenth and fourteenth century, which had consisted mostly of straight-sided bowls. Islamic pottery with floral and calligraphic motifs appears at sites like Manda, Gede, and Kilepwa. This pottery consisted mostly of "small bowls with white paste bodies and floral and arabesque designs, often in panels, in blue on white under a tin glaze" (Kirkman, 1956:96). It also included larger bowls and dishes with the same conventionalized floral designs, sometimes showing Chinese influence or arabesque patterns in blue or manganese black, green, or purple, white or yellow, over massive buff red bodies. Muslim and Indian potters desiring to participate in lucrative East African markets were making Chinese and Middle Eastern imitations to appeal to East African tastes (Oka et al., 2010). This is an important sign of commercial sophistication.

In sum, the late medieval period of East Africa was characterized by unprecedented expansion in interregional trade. Trust and long-term alliance-building fostered earlier among interacting partners formed the basis of exchange networks that distributed goods, services, and ideas and accounted for this prosperity. The favorable climate created political and relational stability that was conducive to investment in agricultural production. Migration to the coast by people searching for opportunities for work, investment, and even leisure occurred during this time, sustaining these complex medieval African towns.

The Colonial Period (1600–1900 CE)

The sixteenth century onward marked the slow decline of medieval Swahili civilization. By the end of the seventeenth century, many medieval towns such as Ungwana, Gedi, Kilepwa, Mnarani, and Ras Mkumbuu had been abandoned (Kirkman, 1957:17). Others like Malindi, Pate, and Kilwa diminished in importance until they were minor towns. A few like Lamu, Mombasa, Zanzibar, and Sofala continued to flourish under foreign rulers (Fagan and Kirkman, 1966:368). The Swahili towns' chronicles written during this period, not surprisingly, recounted bygone prominence and shied away from commentary on contemporary events.

Two new types of pottery were introduced during the middle of the sixteenth century. The first was a long, straight-necked pot with clay strips in curvilinear patterns above the carination. The production and use of this style continued throughout the seventeenth century, declined in much of the eighteenth century, was revived with a concave profile above the carination toward the end of the eighteenth century, and disappeared in the mid-nineteenth century. The second was a short pot with grooves, often with a median ridge on the neck. These pots were made until the second half of the eighteenth century (Kirkman, 1974).

The dominant pots of the eighteenth century were straight, long-necked, and slightly concave carinated pots. By the end of the eighteenth century, these pots often had a projecting lip. Nineteenth-century examples of carinated pots had more elaborate concave profiles. By the middle of the century, the lips had been modified to become squared and chamfered at an almost vertical angle. The most favored decorative motif for all local pottery in the colonial period was incised lines running in semicircles, instead of the diagonal and crosshatch lines on pots of the earlier periods. Serving bowls used during the sixteenth and seventeenth centuries had lipped rims and were burnished on the inside of the lip only. Those employed in the eighteenth century were generally straight-rimmed. Bases were disked or slightly concave in contrast to the ring bases of the fifteenth and sixteenth centuries. The seventeenth century's characteristic water pot was tall and red-coated with a slightly flared neck (Kirkman, 1966:348).

During this period, foreign trade in the Indian Ocean was dominated by South Asian, Portuguese, Dutch, and, later, English merchants. Large quantities of Chinese porcelain continued to be imported until the destruction of the kilns during the Taiping Rebellion of the 1840s to the 1860s. The main Chinese porcelain included Late Ming in the earlier levels and K'ang Shi, *Famille Verte*, imitation Imari, and blue-and-white in the later levels. Yung Cheng ware was scarce, but Chien Lung was abundant.

The smallest volume of Islamic wares was imported during this time than at any other time. The typical ceramics of the eighteenth century were shallow bowls with dirty yellow or pale green glazes or jugs with a pale or light blue glaze over a soft buff fabric. Others included rich green and brown glaze on grey fabric stoneware bowls, and Chinese imitations made in India and Persia. The Portuguese introduced red-and-black polished ware, which was used throughout the seventeenth century. They also imported the blue-and-white Portuguese majolica, including shallow bowls with vertical sides. The Indian chatty, or rounded water pot with a red body decorated with black concentric circles, also appeared. It was imported in increasing volumes in the eighteenth and nineteenth centuries. European china commonly referred to as Peasant Floral ware, including plates, bowls, and mugs, became common in the early nineteenth century. The Portuguese also began importing European beads in large numbers after the sixteenth century. Most examples excavated in eighteenth- and nineteenth-century contexts at Fort Jesus include coarse white, dark blue, red, green, and transparent green beads.

The Birth of an African Medieval Society

We have shown that Swahili society developed through five periods that are visible at multiple archaeological sites (Kusimba et al., 2018). From the Late Iron Age to the end of the medieval period, the settlements' archaeological assemblages were dominated by local craft industries even as the inhabitants increased their connections to the global networks of Southwest Asia, South Asia, East Asia, and possibly Southeast Asia. At Manda, discussed in detail in Section 3, excavations by Chittick (1984) and the author (Kusimba et al., 2018) yielded postholes representing rectangular timber buildings recovered in the lowest levels of the settlement. Material testimonies of these societies' in situ evolution are revealed in the large volumes of iron slag recovered at these levels.

Shanga, another contemporary medieval settlement on nearby Pate Island, occupied seven hectares of stone ruins, including more than 200 houses built in the coral rag. Like other settlements, Shanga rose from non-state beginnings in the early eighth century and lasted to the fifteenth century, when it fell to its rival Pate. Mark Horton wrote:

> These mud and coral buildings are similar to the stone (coral and lime); both contain front courtyards with attached rooms to the rear without corridors. A very identical tendency towards subdivision and expansion occurs in the stone houses. The comparability between mud and stone houses is crucial because it shows that the Swahili stone houses originated in the earlier mud construction. Thus, the elaborate stone houses are a local evolution of a long-established type and are not foreign. (Horton, 1996:300)

The diversity of material culture described here points to in situ social transformations that incrementally evolved before high-volume, long-distance maritime trade and before Islam was fully adopted. Evidence from Iron Age and medieval settlements show the gradual changes in architecture from predominantly round and globular mud-and-wood homes to rectangular dwellings of coral rag and mud and mortar between 800 and 1100 CE. Rectangular structures tend to be easier to construct, require fewer materials, and can host more people. They are easy to expand, and their size is not structurally limited. By early in the medieval period, a cadre of matrilineally based leadership emerged on the East African coast with greater access to essential resources. This emergent leadership would later exert its power by restricting access to crucial resources, both food and nonfood. Introduced toward the end of the ninth century, Islam would become a significant integrative force in the East African coast's medieval cultures. It created opportunities for African converts to establish networks with fellow Muslim traders. Increases in mosque size over space and time bear witness to a minority religion that gradually gained acceptance and became a major ideological factor in sociopolitical and economic matters throughout the medieval period.

The long-established trade relationships between the coast, the interior, and the wider Indian Ocean were dealt a severe blow when the Portuguese conquered the East African coast. The Portuguese arrival coincided with large-scale regional climatic change, which further disrupted the stable and relatively tranquil medieval lifeways. Local and foreign traders who had sailed the Indian and Red Seas for several millennia lost control of the sea and were required to pay high tariffs in Portuguese-controlled ports (Freeman-Grenville, 1973:97). Interregional trade declined, while smuggling raised prices and discouraged or even bankrupted small-scale traders. The immediate victim was trade alliances between the interior and the coast, which were weakened. A substantial number of coastal towns were abandoned due to the loss of revenue from trade. Displaced communities relocated into the interior. The sixteenth-century Mijikenda exodus that created the Kaya settlements was a direct result of the colonial period's anarchy (Allen, 1993; Spear, 1987).

3 What Was the Medieval East African World Like?

The extensive distribution of ostrich eggshell and glass beads at hunter-gatherer, mobile pastoralist, farming, or elite residences in Africa provides testimony of regional trade and of economic and social interactions amongst diverse African societies. Ostrich eggshell beads are often recovered in ratios greater than 20:1 versus nonlocal glass beads. But the distribution of these two ornamental artifacts provides sufficient evidence of local, regional, and trans-oceanic trade networks (Denbow et al., 2015; Dussubieux et al., 2008; Wood, 2012). These networks created unequal opportunities for participants to accumulate wealth.

Innovations in building architecture in the coral rag and coral stones along the coast and dry stone in inland eastern and southern Africa ushered in wealth disparities that were determined from birth (Figures 8 and 9). Fortified homesteads, villages, and towns replaced the dispersed settlements of the Iron Age. Investment and engagement in diverse occupations from part-time, full-time, and specialized crafts and vocations are visible in the various recovered artifacts, ecofacts, ideofacts, and sociofacts. Craft specialization produced a surplus for local and regional markets. By the time Islam was introduced during the ninth century, coastal and inland societies had maintained a millennia-old commercial and cultural dialogue (Chirikure et al., 2013b). As generations of coastal communities' residents converted to Islam, expansion of interregional trade into the interior came to be associated with but was not monopolized by Muslim traders. Although evidence for how interregional trade was organized during the medieval period is scant, accounts drawn from later times support the hypothesis that trade partnerships, known locally in Swahili as *undugu wa chale* (blood brotherhoods), were initiated to formalize peaceful

Figure 8 The Gedi palace (Credit: Mohamed Mchulla, Fort Jesus Museum, Mombasa)

Figure 9 The Palace on the Hill, Great Zimbabwe (Credit: Shadreck Chirikure, University of Oxford)

extra-regional trade interactions and also to protect trader caravans through "foreign" dominions (Kusimba and Kusimba, 2005, 2018).

At the beginning of the second millennium CE, eastern and southern Africa were engaged in long-distance maritime networks across the Indian Ocean. The African end of the trade was financed, managed, and controlled by an African elite. Innovations in ironworking, gold mining, and agricultural intensification, as well as specialization in hunting, fishing, and herding, characterized the regional economies. The opportunities provided by large local and external markets, a relatively good, predictable rainfall pattern, and political stability improved the quality of life and precipitated population growth and economic prosperity (Seland, 2014).

The Emergence of the Medieval State

Toward the end of the last millennium BCE, African foraging lifeways that included hunting, fishing, and gathering dominated everyday subsistence. Metallurgy, and in particular, iron metallurgy, had become the dominant tool technology replacing the late microlithic stone technologies. Increased sedentism, domestication, and adoption of new crops and livestock substantively improved quality of life and stimulated demographic growth (Pikirayi, 2001:80). Ecological diversity encouraged specialization in hunting and tracking wild game, herding, and farming. This, in turn, would promote intercommunal trade.

As we saw in Section 2, disparities in household possessions consistent with unequal wealth began to emerge during the Late Iron Age. Among herders, ownership disparities enabled those with more cattle to gain unequal access to women's reproductive rights, have larger families, and access even more resources (Shenjere-Nyabezi, 2016). Once established, interregional trade and exchange between the coast and inland became the chief means for accumulating wealth in addition to cattle and food surplus. Besides investing in cattle, the elites also monopolized long-distance trade networks by investing in high-value, high-demand crafts and extractive and processing technologies. Procurement of ivory, gold, and iron bloom required investment in ivory working, gold prospecting, and iron mining and processing. These spheres of knowledge – held in high regard and jealously guarded – were obtained primarily through apprenticeship. For example, killing massive game such as elephants and rhinos for ivory required highly specialized knowledge of tracking and poison making, a domain dominated by specialized hunters. Besides being the major suppliers of hides and skins, the emergent cattle elites in southern Africa also invested in the gold and copper trades. Thus, in inland eastern and southeastern Africa, mobile hunters and herders monopolized the supply chains of ivory, incense, beeswax, and rock crystals, high in demand in the Persian Gulf and South Asia. Trade diversified the regional economy and created opportunities for some individuals but also introduced inequities in the distribution of essential resources such as iron, ivory, gold, copper, and salt in favor of individuals who had already built intercommunity partnerships (Chirikure et al., 2013a:341).

The emergence of political and economic elites, ritual specialists, and technical experts who monopolized interregional commerce began toward the end of the Late Iron Age and the early medieval period (Manyanga, 2006:139). Ivory, rhinoceros' horns, skins, and leather were exported overseas through emerging medieval port towns like Chibuene, Sofala, Kilwa, and Manda (Mitchell, 2002:300). Trade across ethnic boundaries will thrive when trust and cooperation exist among potential trading partners. The institution of blood brotherhood that developed during this period was an inclusive superstructure that incorporated all communities from mobile hunter-gatherers, nomadic and sedentary pastoralists, and agriculturalists in order to facilitate interregional trade. Without such a system, products such as ivory and beads – universal trade items consumed by all – would not have been exchanged, connecting the entire region of eastern and southern Africa (Kusimba et al., 2017:71).

The safe passage of trade from the inland to the coast required negotiations and cooperation among trading partners (Table 6). Tribute, tax, and, where necessary, security escorts protected traders and trade infrastructure. Simultaneously, the bulk of the resources sent from the coast to inland societies (e.g., cloth and beads) were circulated to all regions. Investment in weaving was widespread and weaving formed one of the most common cottage industries in emergent city households. The ubiquitous distribution of spindle whorls at most household locales on the coast and southern Africa supports this proposition (Chittick, 1984). In sum, craft specialization in pottery making, cloth making, leatherwork, smithing, curving, stonecutting, and masonry, among others, had become an entrenched part of the medieval African landscape. Wealth distinctions were now measured in one's ability to own and cultivate large tracts of agricultural land, own large herds of cattle, and build an extensive permanent and intergenerational homestead.

Mineral extraction and processing involved managerial organization, technological innovation, and decision-making. The workers' understanding of the geology, their harnessing of the tools – iron gads, chisels, hoes, drills, crucibles, and hammerstones – and practical skills to overcome physical and mechanical obstacles required social cooperation and leadership (Hammel et al., 2000:52; Miller et al., 2000). These activities point to cooperation, perhaps even coercion, and a distinct labor division. Locally consumed gold presumably circulated among the networks of ritual leaders and elders in all societies. These emergent leaders from the ranks of

Table 6 Sources of products important in the coastal domestic economy

	Products	Coastal	Agrarian	Agropastoral	Pastoral	Forager
1	Ambergris	X				
2	Aromatic products	X	X	X	X	X
3	Baobab	X	X	X	X	
4	Beeswax		X	X	X	X
5	Betel nuts	X				
6	Butter/yogurt			X	X	
7	Citrus fruits	X	X			
8	Copra	X				
9	Cotton	X	X			
10	Cowrie shells	X				
11	Enslaved persons	X	X	X	X	X
12	Frankincense				X	X
13	Fresh, dried, smoked fish	X				
14	Gold		X			
15	Grains	X	X	X		
16	Iron bloom	X	X	X		
17	Iron tools	X	X	X		

Table 6 (cont.)

	Products	Coastal	Agrarian	Agropastoral	Pastoral	Forager
18	Ivory		X	X	X	X
19	Kapok	X				
20	Leather			X	X	
21	Leopard skins		X	X	X	X
22	Livestock	X		X	X	
23	Mangrove poles	X				
24	Marine beads	X				
25	Myrrh			X	X	X
26	Ostrich eggs				X	X
27	Poison					X
28	Pottery	X	X			
29	Rhinoceros horns		X	X	X	X
30	Rock crystal			X		
31	Salt	X				
32	Sea cucumber	X				
33	Shark fins	X				
34	Tamarind	X	X			
35	Timber		X	X		
36	Tobacco	X	X			
37	Turtle shells	X				X
	Total	25	17	16	13	11

mobile, pastoral, and agropastoral communities would later become chiefs, kings, and rulers. As a more formalized leadership emerged, the internal circulation and external control of gold mines and the infrastructure of gold, copper, and iron production would become restricted to the economic and political elite, who were drawn into the same networks (Meyer, 1998:212–213).

Mapping the Character of the Medieval State

Archaeological evidence implicates trade, technology, and ingenuity in the rise of the state in eastern and southern Africa. At the height of their power in the late medieval period, circa 1200–1400 CE, these towns, cities, and states were connected to the Indian Ocean's wider globalized world. Like in other states, successful elite manipulation of wealth-creating resources institutionalized social inequality, replacing the egalitarian practices of the segmentary non-state societies of the Early Iron Age.

Many factors, including sedentism, livestock production, agriculture, regional and interregional trade, and crafts specialization, were the catalysts for state formation. Intercommunity interaction improved information flow, and secret societies and guilds formed to restrict access to new forms of knowledge. Migration, settlement, and the assimilation of foraging, herding, and agricultural lifestyles in resource-rich ecosystems created conditions for the emergence of societies that would elevate ritually influential individuals and personalities to leadership positions.

Resource-rich areas with predictable rainfall and fertile and arable grazing land attracted more people, creating investment opportunities in specialized crafts and local and interregional trade. Interregional trade with the coast was a major catalyst in the transformation of inland communities into state societies (Garlake, 1982:10; Pawlowicz, 2017). The managerial elite monopolized trade with rural and frontier zones. The state capitals played central roles as collection, processing, and distribution centers for gold, ivory, copper, and iron sent to regional and coastal entrepots on the Mozambican coast.

The emergence and organization of agriculture, cattle management, and trade control were crucial factors that contributed to the rise of states. But long-distance trade interlocked a regional economy that was already thriving. Once established, long-distance trade became a major builder of wealth and status. Elite control of strategic resources such as rich agricultural and grazing lands, extractive-craft technologies such as ironworking and gold panning, mining and processing, and elephant hunting were crucial for the state's emergence. The Swahili city-state of Manda is a typical example of African medieval settlements that thrived during this period.

Medieval Manda (ca. 600–1500 CE)

The island city-state known as Manda was one of more than a dozen settlements that emerged in the Lamu Archipelago during the Late Iron Age from circa 600 to 1500 CE, when it declined; it was abandoned until the mid-twentieth century, when it was reinhabited. Manda's strategic location in the Lamu Archipelago contributed to its development as a hub within a regional and interregional context. Its study enables us to discern the integration of eastern Africa into the Indian commercial networks and assess the impacts derived from this inter-action. At its height, Manda's residents occupied nearly twenty-five hectares of the island with an estimated population of 5,000 who lived on three distinct estates in the northern, southern, and eastern areas (Figure 10).

The first two estates were located within a town featuring stone buildings, with each community hosting its own mosque and cemeteries. The eastern community, located outside the town, lived in dispersed households, occupying

Figure 10 Some settlements in the Lamu Archipelago, including Manda
(Credit: Public Domain, Google Maps)

a much larger area. Although our surveys in 2012 and 2017 found no evidence of monumental architecture outside the perimeter walls, we nevertheless found scatters of pottery near residences that were presumably built of wattle and daub (Fleisher and LaViolette, 1999). The monumental architecture within the town echoes earlier experimentation and adoption of stone architecture that is now characteristic of elite house forms of the Swahili world (Garlake 1966). The precise chronology of the only standing mosque at Manda places it in the eleventh century (Figure 11).

During its millennia-long history, Manda had a robust economy sustained by active interregional trade and a vibrant craft industry of bead making, cloth making, iron smelting, smithing, and stonecutting and masonry. Archaeological finds – ranging from porcelain, glass, and pottery vessels, to glass beads, to gold, copper, and silver rings and bracelets, to kohl sticks – provide strong evidence for contact with diverse regions in the Persian Gulf, the Indian Ocean, and the South China Sea. Simultaneously, the recovery of local pottery, ostrich eggshell and marine shell beads, bead grinders, rock crystal cores, spindle whorls, loom weights, grindstones, and carved items of bone and ivory reveals Manda's vital domestic craft industry. Both combined to sustain Manda's viability in intercontinental

Figure 11 Examples of local pottery from Manda (Credit: Chapurukha
M. Kusimba, University of South Florida)

commerce (Figure 12 and 14). We illustrate this in Table 7, showing the known exports from East Africa that were shipped through ports such as Manda.

Domestic Pottery: Production and Use

As discussed in Section 2, at 96 percent of material culture recovered at Swahili sites, the domestic craft production economy was dominated by this industry. Manda's pottery was made from fine clay tempered with quartz grains, mica, shell, or grog. Decorative motifs were applied when the clay was still wet. Virtually all local pottery was hand-modeled and open-fired. Sources of clay remained unchanged for very long periods. However, vessel forms and decoration were dynamic and changed as the town grew into a regional hub and became home to diverse residents. Local Manda pottery belongs to the Tana tradition. Due to its 1,100 years of settlement, all decorative motifs described in the Tana ware and triangular incised wire (TIW) pottery types, including line incisions, grooving, and varieties of punctate, including point, shell, and fingernail, described earlier are represented at Manda. Vessel forms, including S-shaped tweaks, massive shoulders, angled bowls, and all sorts of pot bases, such as round, flat, and ringed, are all represented. All features, including ribbing, perforation, and potter marks, are present in this collection. Different pottery types are slipped and burnished (Fleisher and Wynne-Jones, 2011). Other artifacts, including knobs, spouts, handles, and lamps, point to the complexity of the domestic pottery tradition, the consumers' sophistication, and the importance of the local craft industries in Manda.

Figure 12 Examples of Islamic trade ceramics from Manda (Credit: Chapurukha M. Kusimba, University of South Florida)

Table 7 Medieval African exports to the world

African exports	To Arabia	To Iran	To India	To China	To Southeast Asia
1 Ambergris	X	X			
2 Aromatic products	X	X	X	X	X
3 Baobab			X		
4 Beeswax	X	X	X	X	X
5 Betel nuts	X	X			
6 Copra	X	X			
7 Cotton	X	X			
8 Enslaved persons	X	X	X		
9 Frankincense	X	X			
10 Fresh, dried, smoked fish	X	X			
11 Gold	X	X	X		
12 Grains	X				
13 Iron bloom			X		
14 Iron tools					
15 Ivory	X	X	X	X	
16 Kapok					
17 Leather					
18 Leopard skins		X	X	X	X
19 Livestock					
20 Mangrove poles	X	X			
21 Marine beads					
22 Myrrh	X	X	X	X	X
23 Pottery					
24 Rhinoceros horns	X	X	X	X	X
25 Sea cucumber	X	X			
26 Shark fins	X	X			
27 Tamarind					
28 Timber	X	X			
29 Turtle shells	X	X			
Total number of products	18	17	9	6	5
Percentage of inventory exported to this zone	47%	45%	24%	16%	13%

Trade pottery imported and used by Manda residents originated from Southwest Asia (Islamic), East Asia (Chinese), and South Asia (Indian). Two types of Islamic pottery were imported by Manda: glazed and unglazed. Glazed pottery included Sassanian Islamic, hatched or scratched sgraffito, unscratched sgraffito, and yellow glazed. Other Islamic glazes contained polychromes with a blue splash, black on yellow, tin glazes, and blue and green monochromes (Figure 12).

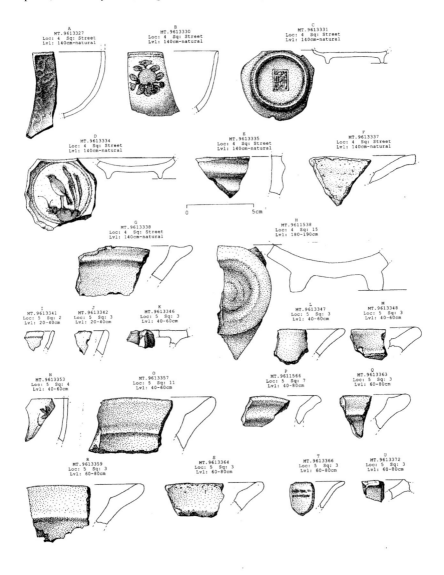

Figure 13 Examples of traded Chinese ceramics from Manda (Credit: Chapurukha M. Kusimba, University of South Florida)

The diversity of the recovered Islamic pottery and ceramics speaks to various sources and the varying tastes of Manda consumers. For example, the Islamic unglazed Gudulia pottery ranged from soft, creamy white to soft, yellowish, creamy white bodies with decorations of grooves, scrolls, molded lines, circles, and geometric panels of grooved parallel lines (Chittick, 1984: Figures 41–46). The different styles in bases and handles point to multiple sources of manufacture in Southwest Asia.

Four types of East Asian ceramics occurred at Manda: celadon, blue-and-white, stoneware, and white glaze. The early glazes, particularly the grey-green (Yue) and the olive green (Dusun) point to the first commercial connections. Green celadon, usually bowls, is present throughout the six periods, pointing to its popularity and resilience. Both the Chinese blue-and-white (Qinghua) and white glaze (Qingbai) in this collection occurs in the middle-to-late Manda period (Figure 13). In sum, commercial contacts with Chinese industrial kilns are present during the entire occupation of Manda.

Pottery of South Asian origin was mostly unglazed, but unlike local Manda pottery, which was hand-modeled, South Asian pottery was almost always wheel-thrown. Indian pottery is well defined by its typical short neck and squat morphology. The bodies are usually thin to medium, except for the very thick water jars or pots mostly used on ships. The dense bodies are generally of porous buff fabric,

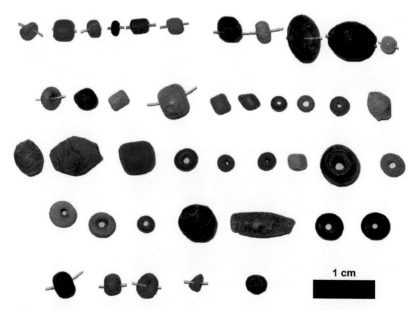

Figure 14 Examples of glass beads from Manda (Credit: Laure Dussubieux, Field Museum, Chicago, IL, USA)

while the thin to medium-thick bodies are of soft fine reddish or purple-grey fabric. Often, they have a brown or red slip, sometimes on both the inside and the outside. Some are also decorated with molds and ridges.

Glassware

Manda residents used diverse types of glasses, including beakers and bottles with straight, everted, and thick rims. These glass vessels' bases ranged from slightly thickened pinched, regular thickened round base, dimpled and thickened on inside bases, and pinched bottom folded ring bases of beakers. There were also incised and grooved glass, incised and scratched glass, a recognizable vial, and lids of bowls. The diversity of glass vessels recovered at the coast speak to the many social and symbolic contexts in which they were used.

Figure 15 Examples of bead grinders and spindle whorls used in making beads and cloth for local and regional inland markets (Credit: Chapurukha M. Kusimba, University of South Florida)

Innovation and Recycling

Many artifacts were modified after they had broken, including spindle whorls made from local and glazed pottery and chlorite schist, and gaming terracotta objects, jade, and red calcite material. Bead grinders were also made from different materials, including local and imported pottery and porites coral. A combined tool kit that included recycled materials points to the diversity of crafts carried out at Manda and suggests that production was at the household level for much of its history (Figure 15).

An Intertwined Globalized Medieval World

The diversity of material artefacts from Manda indicates that ancient trade between eastern Africa and Asia was a complex affair that involved diverse communities. On one hand, Africa's commodities were in high demand in Asia. On the other, Africans were interested in cloth (silk and cotton), ceramics, and beads, among other imports. Consumption of African and Asian products was bidirectional and involved diverse communities whose ways of life in technology, culture, and economics are visible in the cultural affinities of Afrasian peoples from North Africa through Central Asia.

The growth of settlements like Manda, Pate, and Kilwa provides testimony not only to the expansion of maritime trade and the growing economic and political power but also to interregional competition and the development of valued overseas markets. Eastern Africans' consumption of Islamic pottery and of Chinese ceramics and silks, Indo-Pacific beads, pottery, cloth, jewelry, and foodstuffs was primarily through the agency of Arab, Persian, Hindu, and Muslim Indian merchants. The arrival of significant quantities of white wares made in Fujian (mainly Ding, Qingbai, and molded white wares); the use of Chinese and Indian coins; and the close similarity of Chinese green wares recovered at ports like Homs (Syria), Chaul (India), Shanga, Manda, and Mtwapa (Kenya), Kilwa and Songo Mnara (Tanzania), Chibuene (Mozambique), and Great Zimbabwe (Zimbabwe) points to the major advances China had made in mass production technology, which, though indirect, linked the two regions through global commercial networks (Horton, 1996:418). The sheer complexity and diversity of material culture at Manda, alongside the distribution of trade ceramics, suggests that by the eleventh and twelfth centuries CE, parts of the Swahili coast were linked into shared systems of value and prestige. While the temptation to view evidence from Manda and other contemporary settlements, Shanga and Kilwa, as belonging to a larger Islamic elite network including "sultans" with cosmopolitans tastes and preferences for prestige goods shared with fellow elites in Asia and the Mediterranean has sometimes been great, the fact that more than 90 percent of the archaeological assemblages of the Swahili world, including those at Manda, are locally made tells us that these societies were integrally and distinctively African.

4 Global Connections

Introduction

A globalized world is one that is interconnected and interdependent. Globalization implies the breaking down of boundaries of time, space, and culture. Globalization implies our awareness of our interconnections and that our actions, whether motivated by selflessness or by greed, may affect those around us and those in far-off places. This section discusses the following questions. When did globalization in Africa begin? How did Africa – specifically, the Swahili coast – become global? In the preceding sections, we have documented strong connections between Africans and their counterparts in the Indian Ocean and the Persian Gulf during the medieval period. These interactions connected all of Asia, Europe, and Africa (Beaujard, 2019). Philippe Beaujard has traced this globalization to the Bronze Age in his remarkable two-volume study, *Worlds of the Indian Ocean: A Global History.*

As shown in Section 1, the African people who inhabited Swahili towns came from diverse subsistence economic backgrounds as foragers, fishers, herders, and agriculturalists. Some became successful traders with regional and global connections to the interior and across the seas. Still, most African residents remained workers, including some who were enslaved (Middleton, 2004:4). Whether on the coast or inland, these towns engaged in international trade and had a diasporic resident community from different regions. Like their African counterparts, non-African residents migrated for a variety of reasons. Understanding the relationships across these interacting entities is crucial; it must be an inclusive process, not one that a priori assigns current notions of racialized understanding to the forces that shaped global inter- actions during the postmedieval period.

The growth in urbanism between the tenth and sixteenth centuries is connected to regionwide political stability and is a consequence of eco- nomic prosperity and population growth. Migration for work and business molded relationships and alliances that sustained and shaped this emergent African urban landscape. Changes in cuisine and how food was prepared and served are examples of globalization. Trade goods and the languages used between trading partners provide critical evidence for examining extra-regional connections, including long-term settlement and assimilations. Trade ceramics and glass beads recovered at coastal and interior towns dominate the conversation as evidence of the trade relationships and the dominance of Asian products vis-à-vis locally produced ones (Mitchell, 2005). But internal trade and local crafts remained dominant. For example, the quantitative analysis of locally made earthenware and imported ceramics at Takwa in the Lamu Archipelago by Henry Mutoro and Thomas Wilson showed that for every four shards of imported pottery, there were approximately 12,500 shards of local pottery (Mutoro, 1979:62; Wilson, 2016, 2018). The quantity of imported pottery at coastal sites was small and likely restricted to elite uses. So even as this evidence depicts globalization, the context in which this took place should not be ignored.

Discerning Evidence for Globalization

The Swahili coast's location made it a natural gateway and filtering house from which trade items, people, and ideas came to and left Africa (Seetah 2018). For example, Asian domesticates like the banana, successfully adopted in East and Central Africa, were introduced to these inland regions by way of coastal interactions. Other items, such as imported ceramics, remained on the coast as a preserve of a few wealthy consumers. Still other items like beads made their way to nearly every African household, and their story is only beginning to be recognized.

Therefore, the archaeological data recovered at inland and coastal settlements in the form of beads, ceramics, metals, and other inorganic artifacts are only a minor, visible part of these complex networks of interaction during the medieval period (Fagan 1966:93). Inland Africa made the coast "vibrate" with activity and sustained its wealth during the medieval period. It was an integral part of that world. No justification is necessary to include inland Africa in conversations about the Swahili world (Wynne-Jones and LaViolette, 2018:5).

Coastal artifacts such as glass beads and marine shells, including Conus cowrie *Cypraea annulus* and *Polinices mammilla* recovered in interior Africa, provide the best evidence of long-distance exchange (Fagan, 1966:93). Direct genetic evidence for these interactions is beginning to emerge (Brielle et al., 2023; Raaum et al., 2018). Work at contemporary settlements along the Red Sea and the Persian Gulf and in South Asia reveal close regional similarities in material culture, social and structural planning, and urban space use (Seland, 2014). Taken together, these data strongly support medieval globalization and demonstrate that Africa was a significant node in this globalized world.

Swahili Urbanism As an Outcome of Medieval Globalization

The integration of materials produced in far-off places can be a long, arduous, and mostly unconscious process. Marine shells were used in ritual, economic, ornamental, and mortuary contexts, but they interlocked on a preexisting system of inland trade (Bisson, 2000). For example, the circulation of ostrich eggshell beads in the Late Stone Age points to a preexisting craft industry and a ready market for this product. The appearance of coastal marine and glass beads in Africa's interior adds a curious but rare article to an old practice traceable to the African Middle Stone Age. Thus, the appearance of coastal material culture such as marine shells, including cowrie shells (*Cypraea annulus*) that Professor Brian Fagan (1969:9) excavated at Early Iron Age sites like Sanga and Ingombe on the Batoka Plateau in Zambia, points to an elaboration on preexisting African exchange and production systems while maintaining in situ structures evidenced by blood brotherhoods.

Among the trade items from the African heartland destined for the coast were gold, ivory, copper, and iron. Evidence for elite investment in extractive technologies, such as mining, panning, and processing (discussed in Section 3), underlies the regional connectedness in this long-distance trade. Trade items like gold, copper, iron hoes, salt, and beads (ostrich and glass) were in high demand, and their context varied both as sources of wealth and as symbolic status markers (Table 8). Their value changed situationally, and it is anthropology's role to understand these shifting uses and meanings.

Disruptions of 400 years of the slave trade complicate understandings of the history, and anthropologists must resort to employing analogies drawn from oral traditions, ethnoarchaeology, and ethnohistory. Thus, inland East African trading societies such as the Nyamwezi, Giriama, and Akamba, who maintained connections with the coast, provide us with superb cases for reimagining the uses and meanings of medieval materiality. For example, the Nyamwezi trade networks extended beyond Lake Tanganyika in the west, Lake Victoria in the north, and the regions of Ufipa and Ruemba in the South. They monopolized regional trade in copper, tobacco and its by-products, iron, and salt, and still constituted the largest East African trading diaspora in the Katanga copper region in the mid-nineteenth century (Roberts, 1970; Thomson, 1968:46). The trade items served many purposes, and their meaning was also situational. Salt could be consumed, but it could also be used as currency for debt or bridewealth payments. Cowrie shells were ornamental,

Table 8 Commodities of trade between Asia and Africa

Africa to Asia: Goods traded	Asia to Africa: Goods traded
ivory (elephant and hippopotamus)	cloth (silk, cotton, wool)
gold	beads
slaves	porcelain
mangrove timber	rice
grains	spices (pepper, cinnamon, nutmeg, mace)
beeswax	paper
turtle shell	ink
rhinoceros horn	tea
hide and skins	wine
ambergris	sacred and other books
palm leaves (roofing)	kohl and other cosmetics
cowrie shells	fragrance (sandalwood and aloe)
sisal	
rubber	
sugar	

oracle, and monetary objects. Glass beads connected the different currencies used and combined with other locally made beads to improve the "how do I look?" effect.

Towns and Caravanserais As Ports and Nodes of Trade

As nodes of long-distance trade, towns provided water, food, recreation, hospitality, places of worship, and personal security to residents and traders alike (Chirikure et al., 2013a). Trader networks depended on successful brokerage. Intermediaries in Swahili towns assembled crews, sellers, and buyers, giving them financial security to make deals, find credit, provide safe storage, and enforce contracts (Middleton, 2004:79). They understood the climate of the interior and coordinated caravans' movements to avoid the dry and wet seasons that would have disrupted trade.

The risks of trade and safe passage to trade caravans were mitigated by trade pacts, tributes, and brokerage networks with local leaders. Modes of exchange were based upon intimate ties of kinship, friendship, rank, and trust (Middleton, 2004:88). According to John Middleton, the method of trade on the Swahili coast (summed up in Table 9) was primarily between in-laws, blood relatives, friends, and their networks. Exchanges were negotiated between affine within the merchants' houses and secured places that nonfamily members could not enter unless invited – places where open disputes and arguments were forbidden

Table 9 Modes of exchange on the Swahili coast drawn from nineteenth-century accounts collected by Carl Velten between 1893 and 1969 and edited by Lyndon Harries (1965: 182)

Affinal	Visiting Asian trader married daughter of broker becoming son-in-law, matrilocal residence	On the coast, children from these unions became Swahili
	Sons of the broker married daughters of inland trading partners establishing. matrilocal residences	In inland Africa, children from these unions became Swahili
Gift exchange	Visiting trader presented gift before any trade negotiation would begin; host gave a banquet to celebrate successful business transaction; gift, usually porcelain, would never be sold but became family heirloom	Coastal trader presented gift before any trade negotiation would begin; host threw a banquet to celebrate successful business transaction; gift, usually cloth fitting status of the partner

(Middleton 2004:83). These exchanges were not made at impersonal markets (which dealt mainly in foodstuffs), but through intensely personal dealings where competition was carefully controlled and limited. This mode of exchange dealt in relatively small volumes. Merchants sought to minimize open competition. Piety, charity, trust, and religious faith were the cornerstones of these transactions. The affinal nature of these transactions minimized exploitation as they were business between in-laws and the beneficiaries were usually members of one's lineage. Thus the skillful manipulation of kin networks enabled Swahili merchants and intermediaries to control long-distance trade between the coast and inland and to build wide-scale and long-term heritable relationships that connected Asia and Africa.

Merchant Relationships: Inherited Friendships and Blood Brotherhoods

Beyond sustained kinship relationships, African merchants created connections and pledged trust and fidelity through blood brotherhoods (White, 1994). In a blood brotherhood ritual, men would develop relationships, trust, and reciprocity. These rituals were exceedingly common across East Africa during the historical period, as Evans-Pritchard (1933) initially noted, and involved a pact of mutual assistance that involved two participants ingesting each other's blood. For example, the Zandes' lifelong agreement allowed blood brothers to assure joint service and alliance against common enemies. However, the ritual was also common among travelers and traders who ventured beyond the boundaries of Zandeland to trade during periods of hunger or drought. Travelers sought out a local blood brother and relied on him for assistance whenever they were vulnerable visitors. The supernatural sanction would curse anyone who hurt his blood brother. Evans-Pritchard reports various rituals involving cutting the chest or hand and soaking a piece of wood or groundnut in the blood before eating. Louise White (1994) has reviewed similar classic studies and argues that the blood brotherhood ritual allowed men to create idealized relationships with each other outside those already recognized by consanguineal kinship or marriage or forms of friendship with intimates. The blood brotherhood allowed men who had little in common to form pacts of intimacy and reciprocity using the symbolic intimacy of shared bodily fluids. Among the Tatsimo of Madagascar, cloth is essential for sealing the contract of blood brotherhood called *atihena*. One week after the initial *atihena* ceremony, the two individuals united by it exchanged personal clothes. This exchange was accompanied by a telling of the histories, *tantara*, of the respective ancestors. The two actions combined to cement the relationship – both materially and historically – and created a new kinship tie meant to endure for generations. Each piece of cloth symbolized the individual who offered it, while the clothing exchange symbolized their social relationship.

As in other regions, blood brotherhood was the primary means through which people forged trade relationships with each other in inland Kenya. Waata, who refer to themselves as elephant people and live in the coastal hinterland, were known for their excellent hunting and tracking skills (Parker, 2017:40). As Parker recalls, "The Waata longbows, their arrows, and use of poison in the hands of a skilled practitioner, killed elephants quickly and efficiently" (40). They monopolized the trade of bushmeat, honey, beeswax, and poison supply, exchanging these goods for cowpeas, millet, and sorghum with the Taitas' agricultural neighbors, the Mijikenda, Akamba, and Swahili. They were indispensable in regional trade due to their intimate knowledge of the Tsavo wilderness, their leadership in hunting and tracking skills, and their knowledge of the great long bow, *buni*, and a wide variety of medicines, chief among them, that of poison making (Parker, 2017:34). So crucial were the Waata in the procurement of ivory, rhinoceros horns, giraffe, buffalo, leopard and lion skins, honey and beeswax, and other trophies in high demand for local, regional, and extra-regional markets that renowned Swahili scholar Ahmed Sheikh Nabhany credited them with the wealth that the medieval Swahili accumulated (Nabhany, interview 2001).

The Tsavo region of the Kenyan coast was connected by complex systems of paths linking the region's communities to market centers (Figure 16). Local and regional traders regularly met at these centers to exchange agricultural products, game meat, beeswax, honey, milk, yogurt, butter, livestock, and poultry, as well as hoes, arrows, spears, bows, quivers, and leather. Other nonlocal products exchanged included beads, cloth, dried marine fish, ivory, and rhinoceros' horns. These markets served local communities and attracted traders from the region, including the Akamba, Oromo, Waata, Giriama, Duruma, Pare, Taveta, Shambaa, Chaga, and Swahili (Kamau and Sluyter, 2018). Coastal traders brought beads, brass wire, cloth, and fish and returned with ivory, beeswax, honey, milk products, game meat, millet, sorghum, rice, and other products. Traders from far-off places often stayed in the homes of their blood brother relatives. In some cases, the host would serve as a broker, selling the trader's articles and procuring items the seller needed. Blood brotherhoods depended on long-standing trust and reciprocity. The roles would be reversed when the host visited the coast. Oral histories chronicle a landscape of free movement of people and goods, intercommunity trust, and systems of reciprocal relationships that changed in the sixteenth century with the onset of the slave trade (Harries, 1965:182).

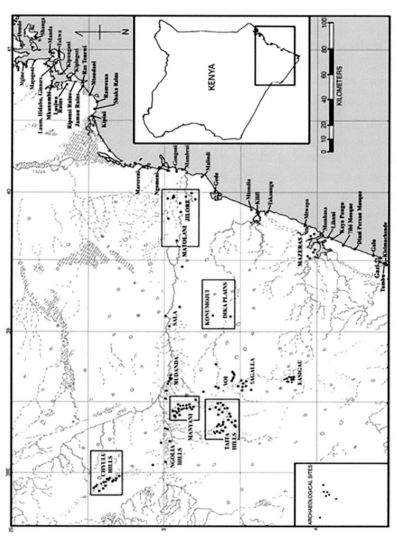

Figure 16 Map showing known settlements on the coast and inland Kenya (Credit: Jill Seagard, Field Museum)

Brotherhoods created opportunities for strangers, competitors, and potential enemies to peacefully enter into contractual obligations that legitimized their partnership with the broader community. Membership in the organization conferred certain privileges: the freedom to exploit resources while enjoying the whole community's protection. In this sense, brotherhoods served to reduce tensions and suspicions arising from competition for resources while simultaneously providing opportunities for access to technical and sacred knowledge.

As Herlehey (1984: 287) writes, the social and economic links between merchants and hinterland communities were mutually reinforced through the blood brotherhood, forging relationships of trust in an area of ethnic diversity: "For example, blood-brotherhood could be used by commercial partners to routinize and secure their trading relations, while local merchants could use the kinship links created by the bonds of blood-brotherhood to increase the extent of their commercial activity over a large territory." Among the Saghala people of the Taita Hills, every man had a Mijikenda blood brother who served as host when he visited the coast and other regions to trade or for pleasure. When his Mijikenda blood brother visited, the same hospitality was accorded to him and his family and friends. He would use his brother's home as the base from which to conduct business and he could expect protection on the journey. The host blood brother did this to ensure that his brother was not molested on the homeward journey – for example, by being taken into slavery. In sum, people put their bodies on the line. Their bodies were their creditworthiness, and through this system, they sustained a global chain of trade that made some extremely wealthy.

Ethnography and oral traditions create opportunities for a counterpoint to what have become traditional ways of representing those on the margins of history, whose experiences are likely subsumed by dominant voices. The relationships developed around blood brotherhood provide alternative ways of seeing and understanding history. Informant perspectives display the complexity, fluidity, and dynamism of ethnicity, identities, and boundaries. These boundaries stretched from Central Africa's heartland across the Persian Gulf to South and Central Asia. Crises and conflicts that arose from competition for access to resources created opportunities for social and economic networks sustained through gift exchange, friendship, intermarriage, alliances, blood brotherhoods, and sisterhoods. The persistence of these extra-regional networks in Taita, Giriama, Duruma, and Swahili oral traditions speaks to the coast's unique global dimensions. For example, Swahili families I have known over the past thirty years have shared their groups' deep ancestry, which they trace to the area of Shiraz in present-day Iran. In their oral traditions, these Shirazi ancestors are the putative foreign founders of many of the coast's principal settlements, a view that archaeologists and historians recounted (Spear 1984, 2000). Current interpretations of archaeological and historical evidence suggest that this scenario is unlikely. Instead, the Shirazi identity may have developed later among the early founding families of cities along the coast as a social stratification component. Social networks enable communities to share resource exploitation risks. These interactions foster the development of spheres of knowledge by particular ethnic groups or specific lineages within those ethnic groups. These knowledge systems provide the basis for interacting, encouraging, tolerating, and even intermarrying with people who would otherwise be enemies.

Medieval Swahili Urbanism and Global Connectivity

The preceding section has discussed the existence of dynamic and complex systems of regional and interregional trade that engaged a myriad of communities from eastern, Central, and southern Africa. This complex local trade predates Islam's introduction and illustrates the regular, continuous interaction and cross-fertilization of ideas, goods, and services among interacting partners and communities. These networks are now only beginning to be recognized and contextualized archaeologically (Kusimba and Walz, 2018).

How might we reimagine how urbanism and social inequality arose from this seemingly heterarchical relationship based on affinal kinship and brokerage? Like hinterland connections, transoceanic connections were equally strong and gained prominence, especially from 800 CE onward. As interest in African products grew in Asia, the Swahili coast and its emergent intermediaries would increasingly serve as a conduit through which goods, people, ideas, and services would move into and out of Africa. Both connections were vital and brought prosperity to the participants in this transoceanic trading system. The coast's unique location was advantageous because it created opportunities for the local intermediaries to manipulate their social ties and networks. Their position had a built-in disadvantage, however: their prosperity depended on their interior and transoceanic trade partners' willingness and compliance (Kusimba, 2018a, 2018b).

Today, the remains of nearly 400 medieval settlements dot the coastal landscape between present-day Somalia and Mozambique. Hundreds more coeval sites are known to exist further inland, primarily in Kenya Tanzania, Mozambique, Zimbabwe, and Botswana. These settlements were diverse, ranging from hamlets to chiefdoms to large city-state and state capitals connected by local, regional, and extra-regional trade. Within these settlements are clear distinctions based on differential access to wealth. The emergent elite enjoyed unfair access to more wealth-building opportunities through knowledge and access to particular local materials. For example, along the coast, members of the elite exploited the abundant, readily available coral while their hinterland counterparts used dry stone architecture to erect their homes. Both techniques are labor-intensive and demand expertise and massive investment in time and resources. This extended beyond building permanent homes for themselves and their families. Investment in local extractive industry can be found in all contexts. On the coast, these contexts included coral mining and lime manufacturing, bead making, boat construction, weaving, lumbering, and commercialized fishing. In the interior, these contexts included ironworking; mining of gold, rock crystal, and other precious stones; and professional hunting of big game for ivory, horns, skins, and meat products. Agricultural and livestock farming predominated. All of these become essential activities.

On the coast, the stone house became a symbol of stability, prosperity, and elitism, while in inland Africa, a stone house on the hill, belonging to a successful farmer owning large herds of cattle or camels, or to a successful and revered hunter, served the same purpose (Barendse, 2016). Access to some trade items, such as Chinese porcelain and glazed Islamic wares, was limited by availability and affordability. However, other trade items like beads and cloth, were distributed and consumed in the entire region due to their portability and affordability. The hundreds of spindle whorls and bead grinders that abound at many sites excavated on the coast show the importance of these industries in the regional economy. Specialization and monopolization of specific tasks by region became normalized.

The medieval Swahili city-states exhibited three nodes of interaction that were crucial for their rise and sustenance: first, the state's relationship with nearby rural fishing and farming villages; second, partnerships with inland communities; and third, the relationship with various trading partners via Indian Ocean networks. At each of these nodes, material evidence connects the state with economic and social interactions that give us clues to the evolution and character of Swahili civilization. Like any other state, the medieval Swahili state was characterized by inequality in access to crucial coastal resources, such as human labor, arable land, fishing areas, and mangrove forests. As maritime trade networks overlay these local inequalities, regional and international trade goods were incorporated into elite-controlled social and economic structures. These three nodes or levels do not have a necessary chronological relationship, and each of them could be paramount in any particular region at any specific time.

The coastal trading centers were linked in urban clusters where different locations had specializations in production and trade. Data from both coastal and other interior sites illustrate the importance of regional, multi-scalar approaches toward understanding early interactions and exchanges. For example, the port of Chibuene connected individual traders from at least three networks: the southern African interior, the northern coastal trade network, and the transoceanic trade network (Sinclair et al., 2012: 735). Thus, the ports' autonomy imparted a resilience to the system that lasted until the seventeenth and eighteenth centuries. The more connection between these ports, the greater chance that transformations in one node will dissipate and be absorbed by the system. None of these ports were a central node in the flow of goods, removal of which would cause a system collapse. For example, the period between 1300 and 1850 CE was characterized by periodic, severe, unpredictable weather patterns that resulted in widespread drought, famine, and disease epidemics, including the plague (Nicholson et al., 2013). This weakened regional trade and cohesion as communities competed for declining resources. Regionwide settlement abandonment and migrations by people searching for food and pasture caused tensions and interregional warfare.

A Summing Up

Globalization on the Swahili coast was a product of trade networks on local, regional, and international levels. An inclusive analytical framework adopted in this section provides a long-term narrative of specialized herding and agriculture alongside the rise of urbanism at local, regional, and extra-regional levels. The emergent elite in the region, but especially trade intermediaries on the coast, manipulated their strategic location as middlemen to monopolize power networks. Like other intermediaries and brokers of the medieval world, they shared the practice of restricting rivalry to the minimum. They understood that their favorable location in these coastal settlements could be sustained by forging and regularly renewing partnerships with the hinterland, other coastal communities, and foreign merchants. These partnerships involved formalizing affinal ties into long-lasting friendships that promoted peaceful coexistence, tolerance, and sharing of the region's diverse resources. Wealth accumulated from these interaction spheres created inequality; this would, in time, increase the social, class, and ethnic consciousness of the coastal region, which increasingly embraced a global Indian Ocean culture while also strengthening its local networks. Ancient trade between the Swahili coast and Asia was a complicated global affair that involved many communities and took several routes that traversed both land and sea. The influences of this international trade are still visible today.

5 Asian Connections

Introduction: Connections with Asia

Interactions between Asians and Africans are among the longest in modern history, stretching back to the Bronze Age. Archaeological investigations on the African subcontinent, the Persian Gulf, and South Asia have yielded material remains that point to nearly 2,000 years of continuous interaction across this region. Relations between China, Central Asia, West Asia, and South Asia in the medieval period were a combination of commerce, diplomacy, and gift exchange. Chinese records show diplomatic visits by foreign leaders into China and Chinese missions to foreign lands between 651 and 798 CE (Li, 2020). Trade missions exponentially increased by Arabian and Persian traders who used the overland trade route via the Black Sea and maritime routes through the port of Malacca.

The exchange of Asian and African domesticates was followed by their relatively seamless incorporation into the daily cuisine. *The Periplus of the Erythrean Sea*, a first-century CE manuscript, shows that the Mediterranean, Africa, and Asia were connected by long-distance exchanges (Casson, 1989). The evidence of these interactions is abundant: from architecture to cuisine, to mode of dress, language, and worship (Abu-Lughod, 1989; Chaudhury, 1985). The significant quantities of trade ceramics, beads, and jewelry that originated in multiple regions of Asia recovered from all coastal towns and cities in the region point to the global nature of these connections (George, 2015:6). The African, Asian, and European worlds were connected by land and sea during medieval times by what historians have called the Silk Road. The overland Silk Road extended eastward into Central and Southwestern Asia and into North Africa. In contrast, the maritime Silk Road began in the South China Sea and Southeast Asia, and connected to the Indian Ocean, the Persian Gulf, and the Horn of Africa. East Africa received trade items from both overland and maritime routes.

The emergence of empires and polities in Southwest, South, and East Asia during the Abbasid Caliphate (750–1258 CE) and Tang Dynasty (618–907 CE) played a pivotal role in the rise of globalization that has persisted to modern times (Kusimba, 1999:1; Kusimba et al., 2019; Zhu et al., 2015). Merchants based in the towns and cities of these empires and polities were the maritime Silk Road trade's main catalysts. Increased political stability, coupled with the trade-friendly policies of Muslim, Hindu, and Buddhist states and empires, led to investments in science, technology, and mathematics. Advances in engineering, shipbuilding, and port development, along with the invention of the compass and the discovery of monsoonal trade winds, increased maritime explorations. China created the first blast furnace (Wagner, 2003). Transformation in ceramic and kiln firing technologies led to the mass production of a wide variety of high-fired porcelain and stoneware that would be distributed all over the ancient world. This era also witnessed major innovations in global finance, including the standardization of banking and promulgation of laws to protect foreigners, traders, and scholars. These advances are summed up in Table 10.

Table 10 Renaissance in Asia (circa 500–1450 CE)

Political economy and governance	Science, technology, engineering, mathematics (STEM)
bureaucracies and tax codes unified	West Asia, South Asia, and China were major centers of innovation
innovation in money, including the use of letters of credit, insurance, and the origin of limited liability firms	thousands of tropical plants introduced in the more temperate regions
new legal status for conquered peoples defined	advances in medicine, including inoculation
manual for kings developed	mathematics and astronomy
tax-funded development projects initiated, including irrigation, road, and shipbuilding	algebra and the concept of zero invented
diverse armies – slave armies, armies based on religion, and prisoners as soldiers	a variety of geometries developed, including solutions to conic sections and even a primitive form of calculus

Globally, growth and improvement in living standards instigated urban development and job creation, which attracted rural-to-urban migrants searching for a better life. Residents of these towns and cities consumed produce from their rural hinterlands and became the primary consumers of exotica from far corners of the world. Connected by land and sea, the coastal sites and their overland counterparts grew into major maritime ports and inland caravanserais (Ray, 2003). Other outlying cities and villages along the chain were collection and distribution centers. All were characterized by storehouses that temporarily stowed goods awaiting conveyance to the next town (Bellina, 2018). For example, Baghdad, from the time of its foundation in 762, was connected to the Persian Gulf by the Tigris and Euphrates Rivers, which lead to Basra, the primary port of Iraq, and Ubulla (the ancient Apologos). Because Basra and Baghdad had ports too shallow for the largest seagoing ships, Siraf, located on the Iranian coast, would become one of the significant ports.

Akhbār al-.sīn wa'l-hind (*Accounts of China and India*), written around 851 CE by an anonymous author, relies on eyewitness accounts of Arab merchants in China, India, and other non-Arab lands. It describes relationships of mutual respect among merchants, imperial states' interest in promoting peaceful coexistence, a devotion to literacy and lifelong learning, fairness and fair play, a commitment to trust, and creditworthiness. In one passage, the author writes:

He who wants to travel from one part [of China] to another needs two letters, [one] from the ruler (al-malik) and [another] from the eunuch (al-kha.s¯ı). The ruler's letter is for the road. It carries the name of the man, and of those who are with him, his age, and the age of those who are with him, as well as his tribe (qab¯ıla): all those who are in China, be they Chinese, Arab or other, must link their genealogy to some [group] by which they are known. The eunuch's letter mentions the money and merchandise [that the traveler has] with him because there are military posts on the way that look at both letters. When someone reaches them, they write: "So-so, son of so-and-so, from [the tribe of] such-and-such, has reached us on this day of that month of that year, and was carrying this." In this way, nothing is lost of the man's money and merchandise, and if he loses something or comes to die, it can be established how this happened or who inherits … The Chinese are just in handling transactions and debt … They are fair in their dealings with each other; no one is deprived of their right, even though they do not use witnesses or oaths. (George, 2015:21)

By today's standards and concepts of privacy, we might find these rules restrictive to foreign merchants' activities. Still they established a predictable framework for trade within China that was replicated elsewhere (George, 2015:24). The practices also reflect the complexities of trading diasporas and how foreigners were treated.

Connections with South Asia

The ubiquity of South Asian beads in medieval African settlements exhibits extensive maritime trade connections between East Africa and South Asia (Gogte, 2002). Indian pottery, including smaller, portable cooking stoves found at major coastal settlements, provide strong signals of activity beyond mariners' annual voyages, possibly the migration of women. In this section, we discuss the relationships between East Africa and South Asia based on work carried out at two medieval port cities: Chaul in India and Mtwapa in Kenya.

Chaul: Ancient Port City on the Kundalika River, Maharashtra, India

Chaul known also known as Campavati or Revatikshetra in the epic *Mahabharata*, was founded during the Ptolemaic period (ca. 150 CE) and rose to become a vital port involved in considerable maritime trade (Sastri, 1927: 42–43). The town was described in *Periplus of the Erythraean Sea* as the first local market south of Kalliena. It exported cotton to Rome during the reign of Emperor Vespasian (Warmington, 1974: 289). Kosmas Indikopleustes confirmed Chaul's prosperity in *Christian Topography* (525 CE). Upon his visit in 642 CE, Chinese pilgrim Huan Tsang discussed the port's commercial and religious prominence (*Maharashtra State Gazetteer*, 1964: 718). Subsequent accounts by Muslim scholars, including Masudi (915 CE), Muhalhil (941 CE), Al Istakhri (950 CE), Ibn Haukal (976 CE), Al Biruni (1030 CE), and Al Idrisi (1130 CE), provide commentaries on the port city's cosmopolitanism (LaViolette, 2008). The city was home to diverse communities that included Hindus, Muslims, Buddhists, and pagans (Figures 17 and 18).

Chaul was one of the several port towns engaged in maritime trade in the Indian Ocean. As reported in *Periplus*, some of the Indian traders in Socotra and Rome very likely came from the port city of Chaul. The Chaul political elite was trader-friendly, encouraged investment, and patronized merchants from many regions and diverse faiths. For example, Gautamiputra Satakarni, a Satavahana king of western India who reigned around 150 CE, donated state land for coconut plantations, encouraged trader investment in international maritime trade, and even issued coinage depicting a ship. A fifth-century CE reference describes an Indian merchant from Chaul as "famous among the millionaires of the great city of Chemul as one whose widespread fame had bathed in the three seas," implying that the Indian traders were carrying out trade in all parts of the Indian Ocean, the Persian Gulf, and the South China

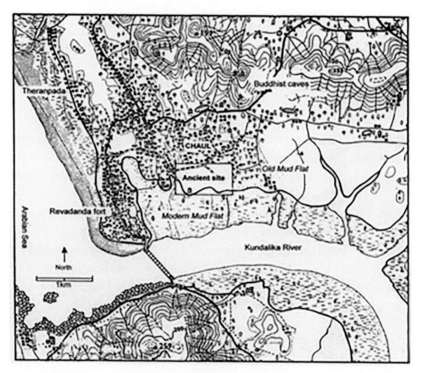

Figure 17 Map of Chaul on the Kundalika River (Credit: Rahul Oka, University of Notre Dame, South Bend, IN, USA)

Figure 18 Chaul had a deep stratigraphy that extended from the Mauryan (300–200 BCE to the late medieval period (1200–1600 CE) (Credit: Rahul Oka, University of Notre Dame, South Bend, IN, USA)

Sea (*Bombay Gazetteer*, 1882:173). Exports from Chaul were shipped to other parts of India, Malacca and Macao in China, Ormuz, East Africa, and, later, Portugal. They consisted of iron, borax, asafetida, corn, indigo, opium, silk of all kinds, and white, painted, and printed cotton goods.

Excavations revealed a deep stratigraphy and a vibrant material assemblage, enabling us to reconstruct the site's chronology from 200 BCE to 1700 CE (Figure 18; Table 11). The large volume of finds included Roman amphorae, glass beads, and Indian, Islamic, and Chinese pottery, porcelain, and tiles. The introduction of the Baobab and bread trees, African semi-domesticates, confirm Chaul's importance in the regional and international (Gogte, 2002).

Mtwapa: A Medieval Port on Mtwapa Creek, Kilifi County, Kenya

The medieval port town of Mtwapa is located fifteen kilometers north of Mombasa (Figure 19). The settlement is situated on Mtwapa Creek, navigable today for twenty kilometers inland at spring tide. Because of its location on the mainland, its

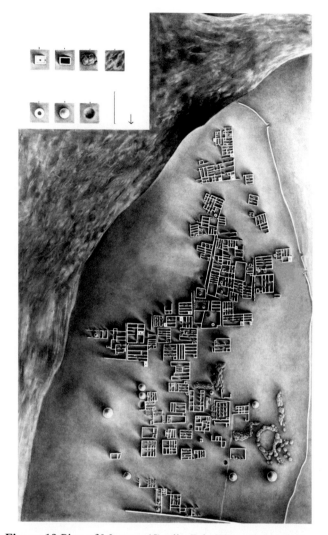

Figure 19 Plan of Mtwapa (Credit: Eric Wert, Field Museum, Chicago, IL, USA)

deep natural harbor, and its excellent landing features, Mtwapa is believed to have served as a trading port for the urban communities of Mtwapa and Jumba and the rural communities along the creek and into the hinterlands of Kenya. In particular, the creek was an outlet for sorghum, millet, rice, timber, honey, honey wax, ivory, hides, skins, and rock crystal produced from inland Kenya. In historic times, the Portuguese used Mtwapa as an entrepot for ivory, grains, honey wax, and tobacco. Kirkman (1964:97) suggested that it was from Mtwapa that the king of Chonyi sent supplies to Fort Jesus during the great siege of 1610–12.

Table 11 The chronology of Chaul

Period	Time	Archaeological finds	International trade
Late medieval	1200–1600 CE	Indo-Pacific beads, glass bangles, glass debitage, coins, Chinese and Islamic pottery, iron and iron slag	frequent
Early medieval	1000–1200 CE	Silahar pottery, Indo-Pacific beads, saddle querns, Chinese and Islamic pottery	frequent
Late Satavahana	230–1000 CE	Late Satavahana pottery, four-legged saddled querns	regular
Early Satavahana	200 BCE–230 CE	Satavahana pottery ring-wells, coins, saddle querns, glass beads, bangles, Roman amphorae	regular
Mauryan	300 BCE–200 CE	North Indian pottery	mostly localized trade

During the medieval period, Mtwapa was a port city of more than ten hectares, with an estimated population of 10,000 residents who lived in several wards, each with its wells, mosques, and cemeteries. Excavations recovered large volumes of diverse artifacts, including local and trade ceramics, iron and iron slag, rock crystal, spindle whorls, glass, marine shells, and Indo-Pacific beads. The town's chronological context, drawn from more than seventy radiocarbon dates, places Mtwapa's occupation by a primarily hunting, fishing, and gathering community beginning from 1732 BCE. Mtwapa's urban phase dates to the eleventh century CE. Mtwapa was abandoned in 1750 CE (Table 12).

During the medieval period, Mtwapa, like its counterpart Chaul, thrived as a port town connecting the regional economy to the Indian and Persian Gulf trading networks. It had a vibrant domestic economy supported by household and full-time craft activities, including weaving, bead making, and iron production. Local potters supplied the city's residents with more than 96 percent of cooking vessels. Nonlocal trade ceramics comprising Chinese, Islamic, Indian, Thai, and Indonesian ceramics and glass beads show Mtwapa's importance in the maritime and overland trade.

Comparing Chaul and Mtwapa

Excavations at Chaul and Mtwapa produced similar beads, Chinese and glazed monochrome ceramics, and Indian and Islamic jewelry. The finds showed that Chaul and Mtwapa engaged in the same trading networks and provide the best example of globalization during the medieval period (Tables 13 and 14). Some of the glass beads thousands of Africans consumed during the medieval period may have come from Chaul or its vicinity and were likely shipped to Africa from there. The cosmopolitan population of Chaul was not very different from what would have been found in African cities. Ethnic and class differences existed, but somehow the populations found the means to work and live side by side with people of different ethnicities, classes, and faiths. Anyone traveling the region during that time would have felt at home in both cities and found friends with whom they could trade, worship, and much more. The data invite us to delve into the meaning of globalization. From the perspective of an East African archaeologist, Chaul revealed some clues. First, the relationship between South Asia and East Africa was much older than previously assumed. Second, trade and other interactions predated the European presence in the Indian Ocean. Third, the view that South Asians ventured into East Africa after the sixteenth century in the service of the Portuguese, Omanis, or British was erroneous. Fourth, South Asians and East Africans very likely traded directly much earlier, as Al Masudi noted, and not indirectly via Arab and Persian merchants.

Table 12 The chronology of Mtwapa

Stages	Time	Archaeological finds	Trade
Stage IV Postmedieval	1500–1750 CE	Stylistically very diverse local pottery, Indian pottery, European peasant floral wares	Regular regional and international trade
Stage IIIb Late medieval	1250–1500 CE	Stylistically very diverse local pottery, spindle whorls, coins, portable stoves and lamps, chlorite schist, Islamic monochromes, Chinese Longquan and Tongan ware, Indonesian Sawankholok or Sisatchanalai jars, Indo-Pacific beads and Egyptian glass	Regular regional and international trade with China, Southeast Asia, India, and the Persian Gulf
Stage IIIa Early medieval	1000–1250 CE	Stylistically very diverse local pottery, rock crystal, spindle whorls, copper and silver coins, Islamic sgraffito, Chinese Qing Bai, Cizhou ware, Bronze mirrors, Indo-Pacific beads	Regular regional and international trade with the Persian Gulf, Egypt, India, and possibly China
Stage IIb Zanjian phase	600–1000 CE	Zanjian pottery: Red burnished and bag-shaped cooking pots, graphite finish, and trellis patterns; Partho-Sassanian Islamic, white-glazed, Chinese Dusun Yueh, Guangdon Coastal Green, and Egyptian glass, carnelian beads, iron, and iron slag	Regular regional and international trade with Egypt, the Persian Gulf, and the Indian subcontinent

Table 13 Maritime trade at Chaul and Mtwapa

	Exports	**Where**
Chaul	iron, silk, cotton goods: white, painted and printed, muslin, copra, sugar, vegetables, rice, corn, sesame, asafoetida, coconut, borax, indigo, opium, and glass beads	Arabia, Persia, East Africa, Portugal, China, and Southeast Asia
Mtwapa	iron, rock crystal, ivory, millet, sorghum, rice, sesame, coconut oils and copra, tobacco, timber, mangrove poles, fish, turtle shells, leopard skins, rhinoceros' horns, beeswax, and amber	Egypt, Arabia, Persia, Mediterranean Europe, Portugal, India, and China

The consistency in dates between Chaul beads and East African coastal settlements firmly pointed to the likelihood that direct maritime trade flourished between East Africans and South Asians. We analyzed representative samples of beads and glass from the eleventh to the sixteenth centuries recovered from Mtwapa and Chaul. The results showed that glass at Chaul was most likely manufactured locally. We found the chemical compositions of Mtwapa beads to be representative of beads that were widely circulated in eastern and southern Africa (Koleini et al., 2019). We concluded that it was quite likely that the high-uranium glass samples identified by Davison (1972) were part of the hU-lBa glass group, which was made in Chaul. The hU-lBa glass occurrence region could be extended to other contemporary sites in Kenya, Tanzania, Mozambique, Zimbabwe, Zambia, South Africa, Madagascar, and the site of Maski in India (Dussubieux et al., 2008:817–818).

Monochrome glazed wares, also called Islamic monochromes, were found at both Chaul and Mtwapa. Islamic monochromes were primarily made in the Persian Gulf and North Africa (Hill et al., 2004; Mason and Keall, 1990; Salinas et al., 2019). In 2006, Kuldeep Bhan made the stunning announcement of the discovery of monochrome glazed ware kilns at Lashkarshah in the Gulf of Khambat, Gujarat, western India. This discovery raised questions about previous assumptions about monochrome production as a monopoly of Southwest Asian and North African kilns. Given the close correspondence between Chaul and Mtwapa, we carried out an archaeometric study of glazed monochromes from the two settlements to determine their provenience. We hoped to reveal the

Table 14 Archaeological finds at Chaul and Mtwapa compared

Indian pottery	Period	Provenance	Chaul	Mtwapa
Mauryan	ca. 300–200 BCE	North India	small number	absent
Satavahana	ca. 200 BCE–200 CE	West India	large number	absent
Roman amphora	ca. 100–200 CE	Rome	one sherd	two probable sherds
Early medieval/Silahara	ca. 500–1200 CE	West India	large number	absent
Late medieval/Bahmani	ca. 1200–1800 CE	West India	large number	small quantities
Islamic pottery				
Sassanian–Islamic	ca. 800 CE	Mesopotamia	absent	two sherds
Late sgraffiato	ca. 1000 CE	Iran	few sherds	absent
Monochrome	ca. 1350 CE	South Arabia	large number	large quantities
Chinese pottery				
Dusun	ca. 800 CE	China	two sherds	few sherds
Celadon Longquan	ca. 1400 CE	China	few sherds	few sherds
Blue-and-white (porcelain)	ca. 1400–1800 CE	China	large number	large number
Glass				
Indo-Pacific beads	ca. 1400–1600 CE	Chaul (West India)	large number	large number
Glass bowls, bottles	ca. 1100–1600 CE	The Persian Gulf?	few pieces	small quantities
Glass debitage	ca. 1400–1600 CE	Chaul (West India)	large number	absent

circumstances under which South Asians began producing monochromes for external markets and how successful were their new ventures into a domain long monopolized by Iranian, Iraqi, and Egyptian kilns.

Merchants and investors often stole recipes from each other to gain a competitive edge. They may also have outsourced manufacturing to reduce costs. Economists have referred to this practice as import substitution. Large-scale imitative production is likely to occur where raw materials and cheap labor are available. If demand for the desired product warrants the investment, production on a massive scale occurs, populating the markets with cheaper imitations. These imitation products can either fill a vacuum left by an authentic product or overwhelm the markets.

Though these processes have been most visible in recent centuries following the Industrial Revolution and in contemporary times with the rise of outsourcing, numerous archaeological cases illustrate this practice. For example, between circa 1000 and 500 BCE, Cypriots successfully imitated transport amphorae (Jacobsen, 2006; Katzev, 2005). Second, between circa 1200 to 1700 CE, Chinese ceramic producers used their vast pools of skilled labor to beat off imitative challenges in stoneware and porcelain production from Southeast and Southwest Asia (Oka et al., 2009). Third, between 1500 and 1800 CE, South Asians used their labor advantage and raw material resources in cloth production to flood East African and Southeast Asian markets and undercut local cloth production.

Investment in prestige pottery has not previously been the focus of investigations into South Asian commercial production. So the discovery that monochrome glazed wares were made in western India and possibly sold to Muslim consumers as authentic Persian vessels was unexpected. What factors prompted South Asians to invest in glazed ware production and compete with Persian, Arabian, and North African factories who had millennia of expertise and monopolies in making and selling glass and faience and low-fired glazed ceramics? (Kleinmann, 1986).

Political stability and the rise of regional commerce in the mid-first century CE contributed to the rise and sustenance of states and empires. Hindu and Muslim South Asian entrepreneurs at this time invested in various industries precisely aimed at these emergent global markets (Oka 2008). Was East Africa one of the markets targeted? To test this, we needed to distinguish between South Asian and Southwest Asian/North African ceramic imports at Mtwapa. Therefore, we analyzed a representative sample of Mtwapa glazed monochrome wares, from the eleventh to eighteenth centuries, through elemental analysis using LA-ICP-MS (Oka et al., 2010). Inductively coupled plasma mass spectrometry (ICP-MS) is a laboratory technique that uses an inductively coupled plasma to ionize the sample to create atomic and small polyatomic ions that can be detected. It is popular amongst archaeologist because of its ability to detect metals and nonmetals in liquid samples at very low concentrations. It can detect different isotopes of the same element, which makes it a versatile tool in isotopic labeling.

The analysis conducted to find the source of the Mtwapa wares, summarized in Table 15, shows that 98 percent (41/42) of the sampled sherds excavated from Mtwapa dating from the eleventh to the eighteenth centuries came from the Lashkarshah site and environs in the Khambhat area of western India, while only one may have originated in Islamic Southwest Asia.

The study confirmed that all the glazes were silica-based, with soda the second most abundant oxide, indicating that the glazes were manufactured using a silica-rich ingredient (sand or quartz pebbles) and a soda flux. The concentrations in some minor and trace elements showed that the recipes of Mtwapa and Khambat glazes differed from those of the Southwest Asian glazes. Furthermore, the Mtwapa and Khambat glazes were similar to a glass recipe developed in South Asia during the second millennium CE. It contains a small amount of potash and lime and relatively high concentrations of iron, titanium, and other trace elements,

Table 15 Average concentrations and standard deviations for the glaze found in Mtwapa, Khambat, and from western Asia. Major and minor elements are expressed as %w of oxide and trace elements in ppm.

	Mtwapa		Khambat		Western Asia	
SiO_2	71.1%	2.9%	67.4%	1.4%	65.5%	2.6%
Na_2O	10.3%	1.7%	12.2%	2.1%	9.2%	1.9%
MgO	1.1%	0.7%	1.1%	0.6%	3.1%	1.0%
Al_2O_3	5.2%	0.7%	6.0%	0.2%	4.9%	1.1%
P_2O_3	0.2%	0.1%	0.1%	0.0%	1.0%	1.2%
K_2O	2.9%	0.9%	3.1%	0.4%	3.0%	0.3%
CaO	4.6%	1.6%	5.2%	1.2%	6.8%	1.5%
Fe_2O_3	1.7%	0.4%	2.1%	0.5%	2.8%	1.7%
B	294	99	363	59	109	15
Rb	124	54	103	19	69	15
Zr	121	34	138	20	32	12
Nb	7	1	9	1	4	1
Cs	4	3	3	1	1	1
Ba	335	129	409	188	318	85
La	17	3	23	2	7	1
Ce	35	5	49	5	18	6
U	19	8	24	3	2	1
Hf	3	1	4	1	1	1
Th	7	1	6	2	2	1

such as rare earth elements. This "South Asian" glass signature is also common to the Mtwapa and Khambat glazes, and both are distinct from Southwest Asian glazes and glass (Dussubieux and Kusimba, 2012).

We concluded that the remarkable uniformity between the Khambat and Mtwapa samples in the significant Na, Al, and Mg and trace element Cr was an outcome of mass production. Mass production usually aims to capture market share by flooding the market with low-cost but visually appealing goods. Aluminum is used for strengthening the glaze and increasing resistance to wear. The low aluminum concentrations in the South Asian sherds was one method for lowering the manufacturing cost. Another strategy was to offset the cost of high-quality glazing by reducing the value of the ceramic body. This is confirmed by the differences in the silica and calcium oxide concentrations. Mason and Tite (1994) suggest that the prized buff or cream-colored surface was achieved by adding quartz and calcium and lowering silica content during the mixing of ingredients for the paste. By lowering the cost, South Asians could flood the market with their monochrome glazed wares and force their competitors out of business.

However, the distribution also suggests that the sherds sourced to North Africa/ Southwest Asia (n = 6) also had similar Si-Ca ratios as Khambat. This might be due to expected variation in the composition, but it is possible that Southwest Asian/North African manufacturers were trying to regain their lost market share by reducing their own cost through changes in quality control and thus "imitating the imitators." If this is plausible, it indicates active competition to secure the East African markets by Southwest Asian and North African producers. However, the predominance of South Asian sherds in the assemblage might mean that the outcome was determined by the commercial advantages South Asians enjoyed over their Middle Eastern and North African counterparts.

The evidence of imitative manufacturing of monochrome glazed wares at Lashkarshah, Khambhat, in South Asia, prompted us to link the production of this material to import substitution aimed at market capture. South Asian entrepreneurs seized market share for high-demand prestige wares in the booming Indian Ocean commerce between the eleventh and seventeenth centuries. The vast infrastructure of production in South Asia, coupled with imperial patronage and the growing pool of skilled and unskilled labor, provided the ideal conditions for such competition.

Hence a desirable commodity such as monochrome glazed wares provided an ideal investment opportunity. First, Southwest Asia and North Africa could not compete with South Asia in cheap raw materials and labor cost. Second, ready customers and markets for these wares were assured across the Indian Ocean in East Africa. We conjecture that monochrome glazed ware production at Khambat was set up with a particular aim in mind: to capture markets traditionally enjoyed and monopolized by the Southwest Asian and North African manufacturers.

The results contradict claims that monochromes glazed wares were made only in Southwest Asia and North Africa. Today, India and China continue to use their production infrastructure and limitless cheap labor to corner manufacturing and service economies. This study suggested that such behaviors are deeply embedded in human socioeconomic interactions and emerge wherever commerce is allowed full rein.

A Summing Up

In sum, medieval trade between East Africa and Asia was a complicated affair. On one hand, Africa's commodities, including ivory, ambergris, gold, rhinoceros horns, timber, and sandalwood, were in high demand in Asia. On the other, Africans were interested in ceramics and silk from China, as well as ceramics, beads, and cotton from India. This bidirectional consumption began during the Chalukya/Rashtrakuta period in South Asia and the early medieval period in East Africa in the eighth and ninth centuries and has continued into contemporary times. Importantly, this study shows that Indian Ocean towns were both producers and consumers engaged in the active capture of potential markets as well as being potential markets in their own right. In this scenario, the medieval African urban growth is seen as evidence of not just the development of communities of passive purveyors of raw materials and consumers of cheap exports, but rather of the emergence of a significant market that other Indian Ocean producers competed to capture.

In Asia, the growth of settlements like Chaul, Khambat, and Surat along the west coast of India provides testimony not only to the expansion of maritime trade and the growing economic and political power of Chinese, Hindu, and Muslim merchants, but also to interregional competition and the development of valued overseas markets. Indeed, along with Chinese ceramics and silks reaching Africa were Indo-Pacific beads, pottery, cloth, jewelry, and foodstuffs. These, like the South Asian glazed wares, found their way into East Africa through the agency of Hindu and Muslim Indian merchants. The use of Chinese and Indian coins, as well as the close similarity of Chinese green ware recovered at ports like Homs (Syria), Chaul (India), Shanga, Manda, and Mtwapa (Kenya), Kilwa and Songo Mnara (Tanzania), Chibuene (Mozambique), and Great Zimbabwe (Zimbabwe), point to the significant advances China had made in mass production technology, which, though indirectly, linked the two regions in global commercial networks (Horton, 1996:418). Comparative analysis of materials at Chaul and Mtwapa, alongside the distribution of imitative products such as South Asian glazed wares, also suggests that by the eleventh and twelfth centuries CE, parts of the Swahili coast and India were linked into shared systems of value and prestige – so much so that different production centers could compete to satisfy these values and capture markets from one another. This conclusion points to the local African elites becoming part of a more extensive Islamic elite network, including "sultans" with cosmopolitan tastes and preferences for prestige goods shared with fellow elites in Asia and the Mediterranean.

However, the same commerce that sparked the rise of the East African cities in medieval times also underlies their decline in the eighteenth and nineteenth centuries and eventual Arab/European colonialism (Kusimba, 1999). By the seventeenth century, South Asian entrepreneurs and traders were extensively targeting East African (and Southeast Asian) trading ports for raw material extraction and as markets for cheap finished goods. The elite Swahili allies of these Asian traders also invested in raw material extraction of ivory, gold, animal skins, rhinoceros horns, and slaves, while disinvesting in local, value-added manufacturing of cloth, iron, ivory, or woodworking. The decline of local manufacturing and the increased impacts of the extractive and exploitative economy eventually led to the collapse of many of the ports and settlements in East Africa. Incorporating laser ablation-inductively coupled plasma-mass spectrometry (LA-ICP-MS) to study a trade item previously believed to have been made only in Southwest Asia/North Africa revealed the sophistication of preindustrial entrepreneurs; the tactics of copying and sometimes opportunistic theft of trade secrets and recipes have a long, vibrant, and enduring history.

6 Who Were the Medieval East Africans?

Introduction

A major area of research in the archaeology and anthropology of the East African coast has been concerned with the identities of the peoples who founded the medieval Swahili cities. How far did their reach and influence extend, and what has been their most enduring legacy? We have seen in the preceding sections that African, Muslim, and Hindu merchants and entrepreneurs engaged in long-distance maritime trade with coastal East Africans since at least 800 CE. Trade consumed and exported by the Swahili originated in virtually all regions around the Indian Ocean, the Persian Gulf, and inland Africa – what Michael Pearson has called the Afrasian world (Pearson, 1998, 2003). Colonial researchers discredited Africans' agency in the making of Swahili civilization, preferring to credit foreign invaders. Postcolonial researchers discredited colonial scholarship claim that non-Africans founded Swahili civilizations. In the preceding sections, we have presented archaeological evidence that medieval African cities on the Swahili coast were African in nature and culture, but they were visited and inhabited by a much more diverse population. In this section, we draw on skeletal biology and genetics to discuss the identities and lifestyles of the earliest residents of the medieval African cities and for the first time definitively answer the question: who were the ancestors of modern Swahili peoples of East Africa?

As discussed in Section 1, the Iron Age inhabitants of the Swahili coast, whose descendants still make up the Indigenous populations of the coastal region, derived their subsistence from forager, fisher, pastoral, and agrarian activities. It was primarily representatives of these communities who are described in *Periplus of the Erythrean Sea*. Their ancestors interacted with each other in the non-state societies that thrived in the region during the Iron Age between 100 BCE and 500 CE. Due to a combination of factors, including geography, resources distribution, and expediency, the urban landscape that emerged during medieval times was one of politically autonomous city-states. They were also oligarchic, matrilineal, and mercantile in character (Allen, 1993; Middleton, 1992, 100). In these early city-states or polities, gender equity in resources distribution was the norm, but women generally enjoyed more social, economic, and even political power than has usually been recognized in anthropological circles (Askew, 2002). In short, these first African city-states were matrilineal. Marriage residence was reckoned matrilocally, with men moving into households led by women. We had here an African world where women were in charge. Although the residents in this emergent urban landscape spoke multiple languages, as their descendants still do today, one language, Kingozi, later known as Kiswahili, became the most dominant. The residents embraced Islam as their religion without denigrating their African ethos, which continues to play significant roles in their daily lives.

We have also seen that like in many regions in the broader world of the Indian Ocean, the rise of urbanism in East Africa coincided with the socio-political and economic transformations that occurred during the Tang-Sung-Yuan-Ming dynasties and Islamic times, 600–1500 CE (Beaujard, 2019). As the gateway into and out of eastern Africa, the Swahili coast was inevitably a beneficiary or a victim of wider global innovations and transformations. Although these transformations might appear obvious, as we have seen in this Element, they have been a source of much debate because a great many people around the world still subscribe to racialized ways of seeing the world, of seeing Africa not as a place for innovation, but as one that receives innovations from elsewhere.

Swahili Identities and Lifestyles in Medieval East Africa

Between 2008 and 2012, I led a team of anthropologists in the study of Swahili human remains that we excavated at the main congregational cemeteries and tombs at Mtwapa and Manda. Excavations were carried out with the express permission of the government of Kenya and Swahili communities (Brielle et al., 2023; Kusimba et al., 2014). We also examined remains from Shanga, excavated by Mark Horton in the 1980s and curated at Lamu Museum. We found that the burial practices of medieval Swahili conformed to the general traditions of the Islamic world: burial with the body perpendicular to Mecca and the head and body resting on the right side, sometimes with a stone pedestal keeping the head in that position (Figure 20). Knees are slightly flexed with arms to the side and crossed near the pelvic area, either to the side of the body or directly into the pelvic cavity. Other practices, including shrouding with no coffin and lack of grave goods, are consistent with the Islamic tradition in many areas. There was no distinction between the burial practices associated with males versus females or young versus old.

The average height of adult females was 1.55 meters compared to that of adult males at 1.70 meters. Infant mortality was extremely high, and most people died before attaining fifty years. This is illustrated in Table 16.

The remains exhibited extensive tooth wear angled to the plane of occlusion that has been linked to agricultural-based diets (Fiorenza et al., 2018). Dental calculus formation was also extensive, with all adults (young, middle, and old) having some degree of encrusted buildup. Age-related tooth loss is shown in Table 17. Tooth loss and ensuing alveolar bone changes were common. Tooth loss usually affected the lower M3s and M2s. Next in the sequence of loss were upper M3s and M2s. The teeth least commonly lost were the upper and lower

Table 16 Age distribution

	Mtwapa	*Manda*
Birth to 3 years	12	2
4 to 11 years	8	3
12 to 19 years	14	0
20 to 34 years	13	3
35 to 49 years	9	2
50+ years	7	5
skeletons not aged*	11	1
TOTAL	71	16

* too fragmentary and/or without skeletal elements for aging

Table 17 Tooth number in adults

Age category	Number of individuals	Average number of teeth per skeletal individual
20–34 years*	16	31
35–49 years	11	26
50+ years	12	22

* M3s in occlusion, erupting, or visible in the crypt

incisors and canines. Within the older-than-fifty-years age category, periodontal resorption reduced the mandible depth by more than 50 percent.

We assessed 102 teeth for carious lesions and found that 14 percent of them had carious lesions ranging from small demineralization of enamel to dentin and pulp penetration. More than 70 percent of carious lesions were present on the cemental enamel junction and between the teeth at the gingival line, a pattern we associated with sugarcane fibers.

The African identity of the coast's medieval peoples was powerfully reinforced by several cultural practices expressed in the individuals' dentitions. One individual from Shanga, an adult male aged thirty to forty years, had mesial/distal tooth filing on all upper incisors and canines. Paleopathological descriptions of the skeletal and dental material reveal a population facing life and lifestyle challenges (Monge et al., 2019). Alan Morris identified an infectious disease pattern best described as yaws in one of the Mtwapa individuals (Alan Morris, personal communication). Life on the medieval Swahili coast was not without hazards. Inspection of the postcranial revealed fifteen individuals with at least one skeletal element that shows fracture with healing. Six individuals, five from Mtwapa and one from Manda, showed evidence of traumatic injury to cranial bones. Five were males in middle or late adulthood. A single older adult female showed two instances of healed depressed fractures. Four cranial remains clearly showed that the injury was antemortem with evidence of extensive healing from blunt force trauma. Two individuals from Mtwapa show perimortem wounds with no evidence of healing. Both injuries are consistent with interpersonal violence associated with these individuals' deaths, and both show clear evidence of heaving with both concentric and radiating fractures. In one of these skeletal individuals, there is clear evidence that a cut wound severed the orbital process of the right frontal bone.

Swahili coast community members seem to have engaged in strenuous physical activities as shown by markers of occupational stress (MOS) and

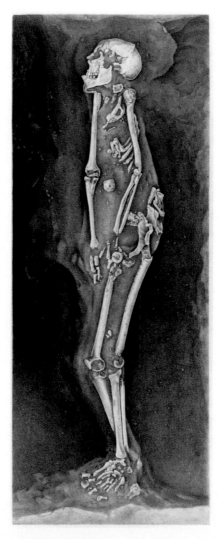

Figure 20 Adult male burial at Mtwapa (Credit: Eric Wert, Field Museum, Chicago, IL, USA)

enthesopathy (Villotte et al., 2010), muscular robusticity, and arthritic changes in joint surfaces. Both male and female skeletons show skeletal changes associated with MOS, in at least three specific patterns (two in males, one in females). This seems to indicate that males and females followed different lifeways. It is almost impossible to associate these patterns with particular activities. Still, observed changes in the upper torso in males are not inconsistent with subsistence activities related to the extraction of sea resources and/or rowing as part of water transportation.

Life and Death among the Swahilis

Swahili life is captured in the skeleton of one adult woman from Manda Island, examined by Alan Morris and Janet Monge. Based on the pelvis and skull features, Morris and Monge determined this woman lived a long life and died quite possibly at seventy years of age or greater. Her body shows extensive evidence of osteoarthritis and osteoporosis that changed her life. Her fourth lumbar vertebral body was collapsed. Osteoporosis also affected virtually all areas of her upper torso to the extent that her arms, especially the humeri, appear to have undergone wasting (Figure 21). This, in conjunction with severe arthritic changes, especially in the cervical vertebrae, limited the mobility in her upper torso, limb, and neck, producing significant scoliosis.

Other arthritic changes occurred in the right knee and both temporomandibular joints. Based on biomedical models today, we know she would have been in significant pain with significant limitations in mobility. In her lifetime, perhaps decades before her death, she suffered two depressed blunt force traumas to her crania bone. Both are located on the right neurocranium on the parietal squama. We cannot determine if her injury was caused by violence or lifestyle, related to her occupation, or accidental. She lost virtually all of her mandibular teeth before death and periodontal resorption was extensive. In the last few years of her life, there would have been no tooth contact surfaces to produce adequate bite force to process many foods. Also, at the left maxillary canine root, there is a large apical abscess. Chewing would have been problematic (Figure 22).

Her final years were characterized by a great deal of pain and limited mobility and ability to process food. Her skeleton reflects the social context of the

Figure 21 Osteoarthritic changes in the elbow joint (Credit: Janet Monge, Penn Museum, Philadelphia, PA, USA)

Figure 22 The large apical abscess at the left maxillary canine root would have made chewing difficult in the last years of her life (Credit: Janet Monge, Penn Museum, Philadelphia, PA, USA)

medieval Swahili: care for the elderly as they age and succumb to physically disabling and painful experiences.

Medieval Swahili Ancestries

Archaeological investigations have shown that Swahili urban society arose from the pre-urban material culture that combined forager, pastoral, and agrarian subsistence economies (Horton 2004:67–88). However, the genetic identities of the medieval inhabitants of the Swahili coast have remained mired in a debate as to whether they were African, non-African colonists, or a combination of African and Asian peoples. On March 29, 2023, the first systematically generated data from more than eighty individuals buried in seven Swahili towns were published. Both African and Asian ancestry were found among the first inhabitants of Swahili towns (Brielle et al., 2023). The data revealed that Asian and African ancestors began mixing at least 1,000 years ago in multiple instances along the coast. Non-Africans arrived on the Swahili coast by the ninth century.

The study found that medieval Swahili populations did not have either primarily African or non-African roots, but rather had them in large proportions. The non-African ancestors were mainly Persian males. The African ancestors were mainly females with origins in different local populations, depending on the coastal location. Indian ancestry also significantly contributed to the earliest stream of migrants. Patterns in the DNA suggest that later Asian immigrants became increasingly Arabian, and they also intermarried with people in the African interior.

Medieval population centers were formed predominantly by African females having families with Persian males who had about 10 percent Indian ancestry. While such extreme sex bias can indicate problematic social hierarchy between the mixing cultures, this is not necessarily a story of a Persian conquest of African towns. East African Bantu groups were matrilineal such that ties through women established a social identity for children. So the sex bias in this study is likely a story of African women and communities in their magnificent stone towns choosing to form families with Persian sailors, traders, and brokers. This mixing between local Africans and foreign Persians happened at multiple locations along the eastern African coast around the turn of the first millennium; Swahili's oral history supports both findings. Some Swahili populations retain this medieval ancestry until the present day (Mazrui and Shariff, 1994).

Patterns in the DNA also suggest that, after the transition to Omani control, immigrants to the region were increasingly Arabian, rather than Persian. Later, they intermarried with people whose DNA was similar to others in the African interior. As a result, some modern people who identify as Swahili have inherited relatively little DNA from medieval peoples like those we analyzed, while others have inherited significantly more. The simple fact that someone identifies as Swahili and speaks Swahili would not, without ancient DNA, lead to any reliable conclusion about their ancestry based on the sequencing of their DNA. The layering of mixture events is so complex we need ancient DNA to learn about the origins of earlier people and their relationship to people today (Kusimba and Reich, 2023).

A Summing Up

This Element illustrates anthropological archaeology is beginning to unveil the rich and complex history of the medieval urban coastal peoples. These people were African but accommodated Asian cultural elements as witnessed by burial practices and genetic makeup. It is difficult to understand these relationships and how they were structured, maintained, and sustained. But we can claim that they were reinforced by intermarriage and religious practice (Middleton, 2004:88). The physical remains described in this section give us a glimpse into the lifeways of these medieval African people. The skeletons indicate a physically challenging lifestyle resulting in trauma, high mortality rates among children and juveniles, and occupation markers of a strenuous life. This is a far cry from studies of the cultural objects that have uncovered archaeological and the ornate buildings in which these individuals lived and died.

In sum, the medieval Swahili civilization was one of the most extraordinary of its time. Its ornate stone and coral towns hugged thousands of kilometers of the East African coast, and its merchants played a linchpin role in the lucrative trade between Africa and other lands along the Indian Ocean rim: Arabia, Persia, India, China, and Southeast Asia. By the turn of the second millennium, Swahili people began to embrace Islam, and some of their grand mosques still stand at places like the UNESCO World Heritage Sites of Lamu in Kenya and Kilwa in Tanzania. Self-governance ended following the Portuguese conquest in the 1500s, with control later passing to the Omanis (1730–1964), Germans (1884–1918), and British (1884–1962).

In conclusion, medieval Swahili towns and cities were nested in larger outer landscapes to which they were socially and economically connected. Settlement patterns on the regional landscape changed as relations shifted. Even as coastal society gradually transformed, it remained integrated into its African core into the eighteenth and nineteenth centuries, when trade of slaves and ivory escalated competition and conflict. Today, this region remains home to diverse groups in the twenty-first century with distinct but shared identities. They sustain and nurture their relationships through a wide range of cooperative relations and entanglements.

Appendices
Swahili Words and Their Origins

Currency

Darahima – maybe from Arabic *dirham*
Fedha – from Arabic *fedha* (silver)
Mapeni – from English *penny*
Pesa – from Spanish *peso* or from Urdu *paisa* or from Hindi *paise*
Senti/sintii – from English *cents*
Shilingi – from English *shilling*

Sailing Boat/Ship and Its Parts

Dau/dau la mwau – dhow
Handawi na joshi – *kamba inayofungwa kwenye dasturi kutegea upepo*. A rope that helps to bring the wind to the sail
Jahazi – from Arabic *jahaz* (sailing boat)
Mashua – original Swahili word for sailing boat

Parts of Swahili Boats/Dhow

Amara – rope that holds the anchor
Barai – *kamba inayotumika kueka farumani ikae sawa*. A rope that helps the mast that carries the sail stay in its place
Dasturi – bow spirit called *mlingoti wa maji*
Demani – *kamba inayotumika kuongezea na kupunguzia upepo*. A rope used to add or reduce the wind from or to the sail
Farumani – mast that holds the sail
Jicho – eye of the boat/ornament in the prow of a vessel
Kaekae – *inatumika kuunganisha farumani na tanga*
Majlisi – from Arabic *majlis* (a place where you can sit)
Mjari – *kamba inayotumika kusimamisha farumani*. A rope used to bring up or down the mast that holds the sail
Mli – head of the boat
Mlingoti/mongoti – mast
Nanga – anchor
Ngama – center of the boat

Omo – front of the boat

Sharuti – *kamba inayotumika kuzuwilia farumani kutoanguka.* A rope used to hold the mast that holds the sail

Sukani – steering

Talbisi – mat fastened around the sides of a heavily laden dhow to prevent the waves from washing in

Tanga/changa – sail

Taruma – ribs of the boat

Tezi – back of the boat

Tumbo/utumbo – belly of a vessel

Uchako/utako – base of the boat (keel)

Uwavu – rib

Tools used in dhow building/ furniture

Guni – square

Kabari – wedge (of wood or iron)

Keekee – drill

Lami – ruler

Msumenombee/mbele – forward saw

Msumenonyuma – backsaw

Patasi – chisel

Pima maji – water/spirits level

Randa – carpenter's plane

Shoka/soli – axe

Tari – handle

Tezo – adze

Tindo – chisel-like

Furniture

Bueta/buweta – wooden box with subdivisions inside used to keep valuable items such as important documents and jewelry

Kabati – from English *cupboard*

Kasha/sanduku – wooden box for keeping clothes. *Sanduku* is an Arabic word.

Kitanda – bed

Kitanda cha hindi – a type of a beautiful, curved bed with different colors that used to be imported from India

Kitanda cha mchongo – modern curved bed

Kitanda cha mwamkisu – simple, multipurpose Swahili bed

Kitanda cha pilipili – a type of bed a husband gifts to a wife as part of a dowry among the Swahili people

Kitanda cha samadari – a type of curved bed made from the mpingo tree. It has its origins in India.

Kitanda cha ulili – a type of bed made from the mwangati tree. It was commonly used by pregnant women when giving birth or used to wash a dead person.

Kiti – chair

Meza – table. From Portuguese *mesa*

Samani – furniture

Foods

Batata/viazi – potato or sweet potato. The word has its origins in the Spanish and Portuguese *patatas*, or in the Arabic *albatatis*. In the Kisiu, Kipate, and Kiamu dialects, *batata* refers to the sweet potato and *viazi* refers to the normal potato.

Bhajia – Hindi/Urdu

Biriani – Hindi/Urdu *biryani*

Borohoa la kunde – thick broth of peas

Borohoa la pojo – thick broth of green grams

Borohoa la yungu/malenge – thick broth of pumpkin

Chapati – Hindi/Urdu

Chuchu – can be made with beans and maize, peas and maize, peas, green gram, sorghum or even wheat. When it is cooked, it is mixed with grated coconut (*ufu*/*nazi iliokunwa*). It can be eaten with porridge or spicy black tea.

Donasi – donuts

Kababu – Arabic *kabaab*, Hindi *kabaab* (*kebab*)

Magoli/mkate wa maji – simple pancake

Mahamri/mandazi/mahamura – a type of bread that is deep-fried

Makaki – a type of bread like *chapati* or Indian *paratha*. Made in the shape of a triangle or rectangle and sugar is added on top

Matobosha – a type of fritter made of wheat flour with sugar or honey and cooked in coconut milk

Mchuzi – stew

Mchuzi wa chukuchuku – coconut milk curry

Mchuzi wa kuku – chicken stew/curry

Mchuzi wa mbuzi – mutton stew/curry

Mchuzi wa ng'ombe – beef stew/curry

Mchuzi wa ng'onda – dry fish curry

Mchuzi wa samaki – fish stew/curry

Mkate – bread

Mkate wa hafushi – a type of bread made of maize flour or a mixture of maize flour with rice flour and coconut milk

Mkate wa jura – a type of bread made of maize flour

Mkate wa kidole – a type of bread made of wheat flour

Mkate wa kijojo – made from rice or maize with sugar and coconut milk. Traditionally it is cooked as a *sadaka* during the burning of a farm to prepare for cultivation. It is also cooked and taken to mosque as a *sadaka*, especially in the Friday morning prayer (*swala ya alfajiri ya siku ya ijumaa*).

Mkate wa mayai – a Swahili sponge cake

Mkate wa mofa – made from millet, sorghum, or a mixture of sorghum and maize flour. Traditionally it was baked in a kiln (*tanu, tanuri*).

Mkate wa nazi – made from a mixture of maize flour or rice flour with grated coconut or coconut milk

Mkate wa sinia – a type of bread made of rice flour and coconut milk with sweet palm wine used as a yeast. It is commonly used during festival times such as a wedding, circumcision, funerals, Eid, or any other type of festival.

Ng'onda – dried fish

Nyama – meat

Nyama choma – barbequed meat

Nyama ya kange – fried meat, normally cooked in a traditional African pot

Samaki – In the Kiamu, Kipate, and Kisiu dialects, it is called *nsi*, while in the Kibajuni dialect, it is called *isi* (fish). *Samaki* is an Arabic word.

Samaki wa kuchoma – barbequed fish with just salt

Samaki wa kukaanga – fried fish

Samaki wa kupaka – a type of barbequed fish with spices and heavy coconut milk

Samaki wa mvuke – steamed fish

Sambusa – Arabic *sambusa*

Shira – syrup (probably from the English *syrup*)

Shurba – a type of wheat porridge with meat and spices. *Shurba* is an Arabic word.

Sima ya mtama – *ugali* of sorghum

Sima ya posho/buru/mahindi – *ugali* of maize

Sima ya wimbi – *ugali* of millet

Supu – soup

Tambi – noodles

Uji wa buru – maize flour porridge

Uji wa mchele – rice porridge

Uji wa mtama – sorghum flour porridge

Uji wa ngano – wheat flour porridge
Uji wa wimbi – millet flour porridge
Wali wa buru – maize rice cooked with coconut
Wali wa mpunga/mchele – white rice
Wali wa mtama – sorghum rice
Viazi tamu/batata/kindoro – sweet potato (Arabic *batata hulwa*)

Beverages

Ngizi – a sweet type of syrup made from sweet palm wine. It looks like honey but tastes different. *Ngizi* can be used in making juices, used as a sugar substitute in cooking, or eaten with bread like honey.
Sharubeti – juices/drinks (Arabic or Urdu)
Sharubeti ya matunda – fruit juices
Tembo tamu – sweet palm wine (nonalcoholic)

Spices

Dalasini/mdalasini – from Hindi *daalacheenee* (cinnamon)
Hardali nyeupe – from Arabic *alhardalu abyadh* (white mustard)
Hardali nyeusi – from Arabic *alhardalu aswad* (black mustard)
Iliki – from Urdu/Hindi *ilaayeche* (cardamom)
Jira/jeera – In the Kipate and probably in the Kiamu and Kisiu dialects, it is called *hawaji*. From Hindi *jeera* or Urdu *zira/zeera* (cumin seeds)
Karafuu – probably from Arabic *qurnafl* (cloves)
Kitunguu – onion
Kitunguu thaumu – from Arabic *thawm* (garlic)
Kungumanga – nutmeg
Kuzubara/kudhubara/dania – from Arabic *kuzbara* and Hindi *dhaniya* (coriander seeds)
Manjano – turmeric. In the Kipate dialect, it is called *kitweo*.
Masala – powdered red pepper. *Masala* is an Indian word.
Pilipili – probably from Arabic *faliful harin* (chili pepper)
Pilipili manga – black pepper
Pilipili nyeupe – white pepper
Siki – probably from Hindi/Urdu *sirka* (vinegar)
Tangawizi – ginger
Zafarani – from Arabic *zaafaran* (saffron)

Fruits

Chenza – tangerine

Chungwa – orange

Embe – mango

Fenesi – jackfruit

Komamanga – pomegranate. In the Kipate and Kisiu dialects, it is called *kudhumani*.

Limau – lemon. The Arabic word is *limun*.

Mabuki/majenga – plantain banana. In the Kipate, Kisiu, and Kiamu dialects, it is called *madhu*.

Matikiti – melon

Matikiti maji – watermelon

Nanasi – from Arabic *ananas* (pineapple)

Nazi – coconut

Ndimu – lime

Ndizi – banana

Njugu – peanut

Papai – pawpaw/papaya

Parachichi – avocado

Pea – from English *pear*

Pera – guava

Pesheni – from English *passion fruit*

Rasberi – from English *raspberry*

Stroberi – from English *strawberry*

Tende – date

Tini – from Arabic *altyn* (fig fruit)

Tomoko – custard apple. In the Kipate, Kisiu, and Kiamu dialects, it is called *konokono*.

Tufaha – from Arabic *tufah* (apple)

Zabibu – from Arabic *zabib* (grape)

Zaituni – from Arabic *zaytun* (olive)

Vegetables

Figili – from Arabic *alfajl* (radish)

Kabichi – cabbage

Mawele – a type of millet

Mbaazi – a type of pea

Mchicha – a type of spinach

Mlonje/tamata – tomatoes. In Hindi, it is called *tamaatar*, in Arabic *tamatim*.
Spinachi – spinach
Sukuma wiki – kale

Grains

Fiwi – a type of pea
Kunde – peas
Maharage – beans
Mahindi – maize/corn. In the Kipate, Kisiu, Kibajuni, and Kiamu dialects, it is
    called *buru*. Maize was brought to the East African coast from India, and it
    was named after its place of origin.
Mtama – sorghum
Ngano – wheat
Pojo – green grams
Wimbi – millet

References

Abu-Lughod, J. L. (1989). *Before European Hegemony: The World System A.D. 1250–1350*. New York: Oxford University Press.

Allen, J. D. (1974). Swahili culture reconsidered: Some historical implications of the material culture of the northern Kenya coast in the eighteenth and nineteenth centuries. *Azania: Archaeological Research in Africa*, 9 (1), 105–138.

Allen, J. D. (1977). *Al Inkishafi: Catechism of the Soul*. Nairobi: East African Literature Bureau.

Allen, J. D. (1981). Swahili culture and the nature of coastal settlement. *International Journal of African History*, 41 (2), 306–334.

Allen, J. D. (1993). *Swahili Origins: Swahili Culture and the Shungwaya Phenomenon*. Athens: Ohio University Press.

Allen, J. D., and Wilson, T. H. (1979). Swahili houses and tombs of the coast of Kenya. Headington: Art and Archaeology Research Papers.

Askew, K. (2002). *Performing the Nation: Swahili Music and Cultural Politics in Tanzania*. Chicago, IL: University of Chicago Press.

Barendse, R. J. (2016). *The Arabian Seas: The Indian Ocean World of the Seventeenth Century*. London: Routledge.

Baumanova, M. (2018). Pillar tombs and the city: Creating a sense of shared identity in Swahili urban space. *Archaeologies*, 14 (3), 377–411.

Beaujard, P. (2018). The birth of a single Afro-Eurasian world system (second century BCE–sixth century CE). In K. Kristiansen, T. Lindkvist, and J. Myrdal, eds., *Trade and Civilisation: Economic Networks and Cultural Ties, from Prehistory to Early Modern Times*. Cambridge: Cambridge University Press, pp. 242–250.

Beaujard, P. (2019). *The Worlds of the Indian Ocean: A Global History*. 2 volumes. Cambridge: Cambridge University Press.

Becker, F. (2018). *The History of Islam in East Africa*. Oxford: Oxford University Press. https://doi.org/10.1093/acrefore/9780190277734.013.151.

Bellina, B. (2018). Development of maritime trade polities and diffusion of the "South China Sea Sphere of Interaction pan-regional culture": The Khao Sek excavations and industries' studies contribution. *Archaeological Research in Asia*, 13, 1–12. https://hal.parisnanterre.fr/hal-01655724/file/Bellina%202017.pdf.

Bisson, M. S. (2000). Precolonial copper metallurgy: Sociopolitical context. In M. S. Bisson, S. Terry Childs, P. deBarros, and A. F. C. Holl, eds., *Ancient*

African Metallurgy: The Sociocultural Context. Walnut Creek, CA: Altamira, pp. 83–145.

Boivin, N., Crowther, A., Prendergast, M., and Fuller, D. Q. (2014). Indian Ocean food globalisation and Africa. *African Archaeological Review*, 31, 547–581.

Brielle, E. S., Fleisher, J., Wynne-Jones, S., et al. 2023. Entwined African and Asian genetic roots of medieval peoples of the Swahili coast. *Nature*, 615 (7954), 866–873.

Broadman, H. G. (2007). *Africa's Silkroad: China and India's Economic Frontier.* Washington, DC: World Bank.

Carneiro, R. (2012). A clarification, amplification, and reformulation. *Social Evolution and History*, 11 (2),5–30.

Casson, L. (1989). *Periplus Maris Erythraei.* Princeton, NJ: Princeton University Press.

Chami, F. A. (1994). *The Tanzanian Coast in the 1st Millennium AD: An Archaeology of the Iron-Working Farming Communities.* Studies in African Archaeology. Uppsala: Societas Archaeologica Upsaliensis.

Chami, F. A. (1998). A review of Swahili archaeology. *African Archaeological Review*, 15, 199–218.

Chami, F. A. (1999). The Early Iron Age on Mafia Island and its relationship with the mainland. *Azania: Journal of the British Institute in Eastern Africa*, 34 (1), 1–10.

Chaudhuri, K. N. (1985). *Trade and Civilization in the Indian Ocean: An Economic History from the Rise of Islam to 1750.* New York: Cambridge University Press.

Chirikure, S., Manyanga, M., Pikirayi, I., and Pollard, M. (2013a). New pathways of sociopolitical complexity in southern Africa. *African Archaeological Review*, 30, 339–366.

Chirikure, S., Pollard, A., Manyanga, M., and Bandama, F. (2013b). A Bayesian chronology of Great Zimbabwe: Re-threading the sequence of a vandalized monument. *Antiquity*, 87 (337), 854–872.

Chittick, H. N. (1969). An archaeological reconnaissance of the southern Somali coast. *Azania: Journal of the British Institute in Eastern Africa*, 4, 115–130.

Chittick, H. N. (1974). *Kilwa: An Islamic Trading City on the East African Coast.* Memoir no. 5. British Institute in Eastern Africa. Nairobi: British Institute in Eastern Africa.

Chittick, H. N. (1984). *Manda: Excavations at an Island Port on the Kenya Coast.* Memoir no. 9. London: British Institute in Eastern Africa.

Comas, D., Calafeli, F., Mateu, E., et al. (1998). Trading genes along the Silk Road: MtDNA sequences and the origin of Central Asia populations. *American Journal of Human Genetics* 63 (6), 1824–1838.

Davison, C. C. (1972). Glass beads in African archaeology: Results of neutron activation analysis, supplemented by results of X-ray fluorescence analysis. Unpublished PhD dissertation. University of California–Berkeley.

Denbow, J., Klehm, C., and Dussubieux, L. (2015). The glass beads of Kaitshaa and early Indian Ocean trade into the far interior of southern Africa. *Antiquity*, 89, 361–377.

Dussubieux, L., and Kusimba C. M. (2012). Glass vessels in sub-Saharan Africa: Compositional study of some samples from Kenya. In I. Liritzis and C. Stevenson, eds., *The Dating and Provenance of Obsidian and Ancient Manufactured Glasses*. Albuquerque: University of New Mexico Press, pp. 143–156.

Dussubieux, L., Kusimba, C. M., Gogte, V., et al. (2008). The trading of ancient glass beads: New analytical data from South Asian and East African soda-alumina glass beads. *Archaeometry*, 50, 797–821.

Ehret, C., and Nurse, D. (1981). The Taita Cushites. *Sprache und Geschichte in Afrika*, 3, 125–168.

Elverskog, J. (2011). *Buddhism and Islam on the Silk Road*. Philadelphia: Pennsylvania University Press.

Evans-Pritchard, E. E. (1933). Zande blood brotherhood. *Africa*, 6 (4), 369–401.

Fabian, J. (1991). *Language and Colonial Power: The Appropriation of Swahili in the Former Belgian Congo 1880–1938*. Berkeley: University of California Press.

Fagan, B. M. (1966). The Iron Age of Zambia. *Current Anthropology*, 7 (4), 453–462.

Fagan, B. M. (1969). Early trade and raw materials in south Central Africa. *Journal of African History*, 10 (1), 1–13.

Fagan, B. M., and Kirkman, J. S. (1966). An ivory trumpet from Sofala, Mozambique. *Ethnomusicology*, 11 (3), 368–374.

Fiorenze, L., Benazzi, S., Oxilia, G., and Kullmer, O. (2018). Functional relationship between dental macrowear and diet in late Pleistocene and modern human population. *International Journal of Human Osteologyi*, 28, 153–161.

Fleisher, J. B., and LaViolette, A. (1999). Elusive wattle-and-daub: Finding the hidden majority in the archaeology of the Swahili. *Azania: Journal of the British Institute in Eastern Africa*, 34, 87–108.

Fleisher, J. B., and Wynne-Jones, S. (2011). Ceramics and the early Swahili: Deconstructing the early Tana tradition. *African Archaeological Review*, 28 (4), 245–278.

Freeman-Grenville, G. S. P. (1962). *The East African Coast: Select Documents from the First of the Earlier Nineteenth Century*. London: Clarendon.

Freeman-Grenville, G. S. P. (1973). *The Chronology of African History*. Oxford: Oxford University Press.

Fuller, D. Q., Boivin, N., Hoogervorst, T., and Allaby, R. (2011). Across the Indian Ocean: The prehistoric movement of plants and animals. *Antiquity*, 85, 544–558.

Garlake, P. (1966). *The Early Islamic Architecture of the East African Coast*. Nairobi: British Institute in Eastern Africa.

Garlake, P. (1982). Prehistory and ideology in Zimbabwe. *Africa: Journal of the International African Institute*, 52 (3), 1–19.

George, A. (2015). Direct sea trade between early Islamic Iraq and Tang China, from the exchange of goods to the transmission of ideas. *Journal of the Royal Asiatic Society*, 25 (4), 579–624.

Gogte, V. D. (2002). Ancient maritime trade in the Indian Ocean: Evaluation by the scientific studies of pottery. *Man and Environment*, 17, 57–68.

Gordon, S. (2009). *When Asia Was the World*. Minneapolis, MN: Da Capo Press.

Hammel, A., White, C., Pfeiffer, S., and Miller, D. (2000). Pre-colonial mining in southern Africa. *Journal of the South Africa Institute of Mining and Metallurgy*, 100, 49–56.

Harries, L. (1965). *Swahili Prose Texts: A Selection from the Material Collected by Carl Velten from 1893 to 1896*. London: Oxford University Press.

Helm, R., Crowther, A., Shipton, C., et al. (2012). Exploring agriculture, interaction and trade on the eastern African littoral: Preliminary results from Kenya. *Azania: Archaeological Research in Africa*, 47 (1), 39–63.

Herlehey, T. J. (1984). Ties that bind. *International Journal of African Historical Studies* 17 (2), 285–308.

Hill, D. V., Speakman, R. J., Glasscock, M. D. (2004). Chemical and mineralogical characterization of Sassanian and early Islamic glazed ceramics from the Deh Luran plain, southwest Iran. *Archaeometry*, 46 (4), 585–605.

Horton, M. C. (1984). The Early Settlement of the Northern Swahili Coast. PhD dissertation. University of Cambridge.

Horton, M. C. (1996). *Shanga: The Archaeology of a Muslim Trading Community on the Coast of East Africa*. Memoirs of the British Institute in Eastern Africa 14. London: British Institute in Eastern Africa.

Horton, M. C. (2004). Islam, archaeology and identity. In D. Whitcomb, ed., *Changing Social Identity with the Spread of Islam*. Chicago, IL: Oriental Institute of the University of Chicago, pp. 67–88.

Horton, M. C., and Chami, F. A. (2018). Swahili origins. In S. Wynne-Jones and A. LaViolette, eds., *The Swahili World*. New York: Routledge/Taylor and Francis, pp. 135–146.

Ichumbaki, E. B., and Pollard, E. (2015). Valuing the Swahili cultural heritage: A Maritime Cultural Ecosystem Services Study from Kilwa, Tanzania. *Conservation and Management of Archaeological Sites*, 21 (4), 230–255.

Jacobsen, W. (2006). Transport amphorae. In W. L. Sorensen and W. K. Jacobsen, eds., *Panayia Ematousa I: A Rural Site in South-eastern Cyprus*. Aarhus: Danish Institute at Athens, pp. 303–307.

Katzev, S. (2005). Resurrecting an ancient Greek ship: Kyrenia, Cyprus, In G. F. Bass, ed., *Beneath the Seven Seas: Adventures with the Institute of Nautical Archaeology*. London: Thames and Hudson, pp. 72–79.

Kirkman, J. S. (1956). The culture of the Kenya coast in the later Middle Ages: Some conclusions from excavations 1948–56. *South African Archaeological Bulletin*, 11 (44), 89–99.

Kirkman, J. S. (1957). Historical archaeology in Kenya 1948–1956. *Antiquaries Journal*, 37, 16–29.

Kirkman, J. S. (1963). *Gedi: The Palace*. The Hague: Mouton.

Kirkman, J. S. (1964). *Men and Monuments on the East African Coast*. London: Lutterworth Press.

Kirkman, J. S. (1966). *Ungwana on the Tana: Studies in African History, Anthropology and Ethnology*. The Hague: Mouton.

Kirkman, J. S. (1974). *Fort Jesus: A Portuguese Fortress on the East African Coast*. Oxford: Clarendon.

Kleinmann, B. (1986). History and development of early Islamic pottery glazes. In J. Olin and M. J. Blackman, eds., *Proceedings of the 24th International Archaeometry Symposium*. Washington, DC: Smithsonian Institution Press, pp. 73–84.

Koleini, F., Colomban, P., Pikirayi, I., and Prinsloo, L. (2019). Glass beads, markers of ancient trade in sub-Saharan Africa: Methodology, state of the art and perspectives. *Heritage*, 2, 2343–2369.

Kusimba, C. M. (1999). *The Rise and Fall of Swahili States*. Walnut Creek, CA: Altamira.

Kusimba, C. M. (2017). The Swahili and globalization in the Indian Ocean. In T. Hodos, ed., *The Routledge Handbook of Archaeology and Globalization*. London: Routledge, pp. 104–122.

Kusimba, C. M. (2018a). Trade and the medieval Swahili state. In J. L. Brook, ed., *State Formations: Histories and Cultures of State*. Cambridge: Cambridge University Press, pp. 90–107.

Kusimba, C. M. (2018b). Trade and civilization in medieval East Africa: Socioeconomic networks. In K. Kristiansen, T. Lindkvist, and J. Myrdal, eds., *Ancient Trade and Civilization*. Cambridge University Press, Cambridge, pp. 320–353.

Kusimba, C. M., Killick, D., and Creswell, R. G. (1994). Indigenous and imported metals in Swahili sites on the Kenyan coast. *MASCA Research Papers in Science and Archaeology*, 11, 63–78.

Kusimba, C. M., and Kusimba, S. B. (2005). Mosaics and interactions: East Africa, 2000 B.P. to the present. In A. B. Stahl, ed., *African Archaeology*. Oxford: Blackwell, pp. 392–419.

Kusimba, C. M., and Kusimba, S. B. (2018). Mosaics: Rethinking African connections in coastal and hinterland relationships. In S. Wynne-Jones and A. LaViolette, eds., *The Swahili World*. London: Routledge, pp. 403–418.

Kusimba, C. M., Kusimba, S. B., and Dussubieux, L. (2013). Beyond the coastalscapes: Preindustrial social and political networks in East Africa. *African Archaeological Review*, 30, 39–63.

Kusimba, C. M., Kusimba, S. B., and Wright, D. K. (2005). The collapse of the Tsavo Mosaic. *Journal of African Archaeology*, 3 (2), 243–265.

Kusimba, C. M., Monge, J., and Kusimba, S. B. (2014). The identity of early Kenyan Coastal peoples: A comparative analysis of human remains from Shanga, Mtwapa, and the Taita Hills. In R. Gearhart and L. Giles, eds., *Contested Identities: The Mijikenda and Their Neighbors in Kenyan Coastal Society*. Trenton, NJ: African World Press, pp. 3–24.

Kusimba, C. M., Nam K., and Kusimba, S. B. (2017). Trade and state formation on the ancient East African and Southern Zambezia. In R. J. Chacon and R. G. Mendoza, eds., *Feast, Famine or Fighting? Multiple Pathways to Social Complexity*. New York: Springer, pp. 61–89.

Kusimba, C. M., and Reich, D. (2023). Ancient DNA is restoring the origin history of the Swahili of East Africa. *The Conversation*, March 29. https://theconversation.com/ancient-dna-is-restoring-the-origin-story-of-the-swahili-people-of-the-east-african-coast-201154.

Kusimba, C. M., and Walz, J. (2018). When did the Swahili become maritime? A reply to Fleisher et al. (2015), and to the resurgence of maritime myopia in the archaeology of the Swahili coast. *American Anthropologist*, 120 (3), 429–443.

Kusimba, C. M., Zhu, T., and Kiura, P. W. (2019). *China and East Africa: Ancient Ties, Contemporary Flows*. Lanham, MD: Lexington Books.

LaViolette, A. (2008). Swahili cosmopolitanism in Africa and the Indian Ocean world, AD 600–1500. *Archaeologies*, 4 (1), 24–49.

LaViolette, A., and Fleischer, J. (2005). The Swahili. In A. B. Stahl, ed., *African Archaeology*. Boston, MA: Blackwell, pp. 392–419.

Li, X. (2020). Six hundred years of harmony: Comparing Zheng He's west ocean navigation with China's African policy. In C. M. Kusimba, T. Zhu, and P. W. Kiura, eds., *China and East Africa: Ancient Ties and Contemporary Flows*. Lanham, MD: Lexington Books, pp. 167–186.

Maharashtra State Gazetteer (1964). *District Kolaba*. Maharashtra State Gazetteers. Bombay: Directorate of Printing and Stationery.

Manyanga, M. (2006). *Resilient Landscapes: Socio-environmental Dynamics in the Shashi–Limpopo Basin, Southern Zimbabwe c. AD 800 to the Present*. Studies in African Archaeology. Uppsala: Societas Archaeologica Upsaliensis.

Mapunda, B. B. (1995). *Iron Age Archaeology in the Southeastern Lake Tanganyika Region, Southwestern Tanzania*. PhD dissertation. Gainesville: University of Florida.

Mason, R. B., and Keall, E. J. (1990). Petrography of Islamic pottery from Fustat. *Journal of the American Research Center in Egypt*, 27, 165–184.

Mason, R. B., and Tite, M. S. (1994). The beginnings of Islamic stone paste technology. *Archaeometry*, 36 (1), 77–91.

Mathew, G. (1956). The culture of the East African coast in the 17th and 18th centuries in the light of recent archaeological discoveries. *Man*, 56, 65–68.

Mazrui, A. M., and Shariff, I. N. (1994). *The Swahili: Idiom and Identity of an African People*. Trenton, NJ: Africa World Press.

Meier, P. (2016). *Swahili Port Cities: The Architecture from Elsewhere*. Bloomington: Indiana University Press.

Meyer, A. (1998). *The Archaeological Sites of Greefswald*. Pretoria: University of Pretoria Press.

Middleton, J. (1992). *The World of the Swahili*. New Haven, CT: Yale University Press.

Middleton, J. (2004). *African Merchants of the Indian Ocean: Swahili of the East African Coast*. Long Grove, IL: Waveland Press.

Miller, D., Desai, N., and Lee-Thorp, J. (2000). Indigenous gold mining in southern Africa: A review. *South African Archaeological Bulletin Goodwin Series,* 8, 91–99.

Mitchell, P. (2002). *The Archaeology of Southern Africa*. Cambridge: Cambridge University Press.

Mitchell, P. (2005). *African Connections: Archaeological Perspectives on Africa and the Wider World*. Walnut Creek, CA: Altamira.

Mkilifi, A. M. H. (1972). Triglossia and Swahili English Bilingualism in Tanzania. *Language in Society*, 1 (2), 197–213.

Monge, J., Morris, A., Williams, S., and Kusimba, C. M. (2019). Life, death, and identity of the early Swahili peoples of the Kenyan coast. In C. M. Kusimba, T. Zhu, and P. W. Kiura, eds., *China and East Africa: Ancient Ties, Contemporary Flows*. Lanham, MD: Lexington Books, pp. 65–85.

Mutoro, H. W. (1979). *A Contribution to the Study of the Cultural and Economic Dynamics of the Historical Settlements of East African Coast with Particular Reference to Takwa Ruins North Kenya Coast*. M.A. thesis, University of Nairobi.

Mutoro, H. W. (1987). *An Archaeological Study of the Mijikenda Kaya Settlement*. PhD thesis, University of California – Los Angeles.

Nabhany, A. S. (2001). Personal interview. Fort Jesus Museum, Mombasa.

Nicholson, S. E., Nash, D. J., Chase, B. M., et al. (2013). Temperature variability over Africa during the last 2000 years. *Holocene*, 23, 1085–1094.

Nurse, D. (1983). History from linguistics: The case of the Tana River. *History in Africa* 10, 207–238.

Nurse, D., and Hinnesbusch, T. (1993). *Swahili and Sabaki: A Linguistic History*. Berkeley: University of California Press.

Nurse, D., and Spear, T. (1985). *The Swahili: Reconstructing the History and Language of an African Society 800–1500*. Philadelphia: University of Pennsylvania Press.

Oka, R. C. (2008). *Resilience and Adaptation of Trade Networks in East African and South Asian Port Polities, 1500–1800 CE*. Doctoral thesis. Chicago: University of Illinois at Chicago.

Oka, R. C. (2018). Trade, traders, and trading systems: Macromodeling of trade, commerce, and civilization in the Indian Ocean. In K. Kristiansen, T. Lindkvist, and J. Myrdal, eds., *Trade and Civilisation: Economic Networks and Cultural Ties, from Prehistory to Early Modern Times*. Cambridge: Cambridge University Press, pp. 279–319.

Oka, R., Dussubieux L., Kusimba, C. M., and Gogte, V. (2009). The impact of imitation ceramic industries and internal political restrictions on Chinese ceramic exports in the Indian Ocean maritime exchange. In Ann S. Grogg, ed., *Scientific Research on Historic Asian Ceramics: Proceedings of the Fourth Forbes Symposium at the Freer Gallery of Art*. Washington, DC: Freer Art Gallery of Art, Smithsonian Institution, pp. 75–185.

Oka, R. C., and Kusimba, C. M. (2008). Archaeology of trading systems 1: A theoretical survey. *Journal of Archaeological Research*, 16, 339–395.

Oka, R. C., Kusimba, C. M., and Gogte, V. D. (2009). Where others fear to *trade*: Modeling adaptive resilience in ethnic trading networks to famines, maritime warfare and imperial stability in the growing Indian Ocean economy, ca. 1500–1700 CE. In E. C. Jones and A. D. Murphy, eds., *The Political Economy of Hazards and Disasters*. Walnut Creek, CA: Altamira, pp. 201–240.

Oteyo, G., and Kusimba, C. M. (2019). The consumption of beads in ancient Swahili East Africa. In C. M. Kusimba, T. Zhu, and P. W. Kiura, eds., *China and East Africa: Ancient Ties, Contemporary Flows*. Lanham, MD: Lexington Books, pp. 147–164.

Ousley, S., Jantz, R., and Freid, D. (2009). Understanding race and human variation: Why forensic anthropologists are good at identifying race. *American Journal of Physical Anthropology*, 139, 68–76.

Parker, I. (2017). Bows, arrows, poison, and elephants. *Kenya Past and Present*, 44, 31–44.

Pawlowicz, M. (2017). *Archaeological Survey and Excavations at Mikindani, Southern Tanzania: Finding Their Place in the Swahili World*. BAR International Series. Oxford: Oxford University Press.

Pearson, M. N. (1998). *Port Cities and Intruders: The Swahili Coast, India, and Portugal in the Early Modern Era*. Baltimore, MD: Johns Hopkins University Press.

Pearson, M. N. (2003). *The Indian Ocean*. New York: Routledge.

Perkins, J., Fleisher, J., and Wynne-Jones, S. (2014). A deposit of Kilwa-type coins from Songo Mnara, Tanzania. *Archaeological Research in Africa*, 49 (1), 102–116.

Phillipson, D. W. (1977). *The Later Prehistory of Eastern and Southern Africa*. Portsmouth: Heinemann Educational.

Pikirayi, I. (2001). *The Zimbabwe Culture: Origins and Decline of Southern Zambezian States*. Walnut Creek, CA: Altamira.

Pouwels, R. L. (1987). *Horn and Crescent: Cultural Change and Traditional Islam on the East African Coast, 800–1900*. Cambridge: Cambridge University Press.

Raaum, R. L., Williams, S. R., Kusimba, C. M., et al. (2018). Decoding the genetic ancestry of the Swahili. In S. Wynne-Jones and A. LaViolette, eds., *The Swahili World*. New York: Routledge/Taylor and Francis, pp. 81–102.

Ray, H. P. (2003). *The Archaeology of Seafaring in Ancient South Asia*. Cambridge: Cambridge University Press.

Roberts, A. D. (1970). Nyamwezi trade. In R. Gray and D. Birmingham, eds., *Pre-colonial African Trade: Essays on Trade in Central and Eastern Africa before 1900*. London: Cambridge University Press, pp. 649–701.

Rothman, N. C. (2002). Indian Ocean trading links: The Swahili experience. *Comparative Civilizations Review*, 46 (46), 1–13.

Rowland, M., and Fuller, D. Q. (2018). In K. Kristiansen, T. Lindkvist, and J. Myrdal, eds., *Trade and Civilisation: Economic Networks and Cultural Ties, from Prehistory to Early Modern Times*. Cambridge: Cambridge University Press, pp. 279–319.

Salim, A. I. (1985). The elusive "Mswahili": Some reflections on his identity and culture. In J. Maw and D. Parkin, eds., *Swahili Language and Society*. Vienna: Beiträge Zur Afrikanistik, pp. 23, 215–228.

Salinas, E., Pradell, T., and Molera, J. (2019). Glaze production at an early Islamic workshop in al-Andalus. *Journal of Archaeological and Anthropological Science*, 11, 2201–2213.

Sanseverino, H. C. (1983). Archaeological remains on the southern Somali coast. *Azania: Archaeological Research in Africa*, 18 (1), 151–164.

Sarathi, A. (2015). Early maritime cultures in East Africa and the western Indian Ocean. Oxford: Archaeopress.

Sastri, S. M. (1927). *McCrindle's Ancient India As Described by Ptolemy*. Calcutta: Chuckervertty, Chatterjee and Company.

Seetah, K. (2018). *Connecting Continents: Archaeology and History in the Indian Ocean World*. Athens: Ohio University Press.

Seland, E. H. (2014). Archaeology of trade in the western Indian Ocean, 300 BC–AD 700. *Journal of Archaeological Research*, 22, 367–402.

Shenjere-Nyabezi, P. (2016). Imperceptible realities: An ethnoarchaeological perspective on the acquisition, ownership, and management of cattle by women in southeastern Zimbabwe. *Azania: Archaeological Research in Africa*, 51 (3), 380–402.

Sinclair, P. J. J., Ekblom, A., and Wood, M. (2012). Trade and society on the south-east African coast in the later first millennium AD: The case of Chibuene. *Antiquity*, 86, 723–737.

Soper, R. (1971). Early Iron Age pottery types from East Africa: Comparative analysis. *Azania: Archaeological Research in Africa*, 6 (1),39–52.

Spear, T. (1984). The Shirazi in Swahili traditions, culture, and history. *History in Africa*, 11, 291–305.

Spear, T. (1987). The interpretation of evidence in African history. *African Studies Review*, 30 (2), 17–24.

Spear, T. (2000). Early Swahili history reconsidered. *International Journal of African Historical Studies*, 33, 257–290.

Stanish, C. S. (2017). *Evolution of Cooperation*. Cambridge: Cambridge University Press.

Stiles, D. (1981). Hunters of the northern East African coast: Origins and historical processes. *Africa*, 51 (4), 828–862.

Thomson, J. (1968). *To the Central African Lakes and Back: The Narrative of the Royal Geographical Society's East Central African Expedition 1878–1880* (orig. ed. London, 1881). London: Searle.

Verin, P. (1986). The history of civilisation in north Madagascar. London: Routledge.

Villotte, S. D., Castex, V., Couallier, V., et al. (2010). Enthesopathies as occupational stress markers: Evidence from the upper limb. *American Journal of Physical Anthropology*, 142 (2), 224–234.

Wagner, D. B. (2003). Chinese blast furnaces from the 10th to the 14th century. *Historical Metallurgy*, 37, 25–37.

Walshaw, S. (2015). *Swahili Trade, Urbanization, and Food Production: Botanical Perspectives from Pemba Island, Tanzania, AD 700–1500*. BAR. Cambridge Monographs in African Archaeology. Oxford: Archaeopress.

Walz, J. R. (2009). Archaeologies of disenchantment. In Peter Schmidt, ed., *Postcolonial Archaeologies of Africa*. Santa Fe, NM: School for Advanced Research Press, pp. 21–38.

Walz, J. R. (2013). Routes to history: Archaeology and being articulate in eastern Africa. In P. Schmidt and S. Mrozowski, eds.,*The Death of Prehistory*. Oxford: Oxford University Press, pp. 69–91.

Warmington, E. H. (1974). *The Commerce between the Roman Empire and India*. New Delhi: Vikas.

White, L. (1994). Blood brotherhood revisited: Kinship, relationship, and the body in East and Central Africa. *Africa*, 64 (3), 359–372.

Wilson, T. H. (2016). *The Monumental Architecture and Archaeology of the Northern Kenya Coast*. Nairobi: National Museums of Kenya.

Wilson, T. H. (2018). *Southern Kenya Coast*. Nairobi: National Museums of Kenya.

Wood, M. (2012). *Interconnections: Glass Beads and Trade in Southern and Eastern Africa and the Indian Ocean, 7th to 16th centuries AD*. Uppsala: Department of Archaeology and Ancient History.

Wynne-Jones, S. (2014). Africa's emporia. In S. M. Sindbaek and A. Trakadas, eds., *The World of the Viking Age*. Roskilde: Viking Ship Museum, pp. 50–53.

Wynne-Jones, S., and LaViolette, A. (2018). *The Swahili World*. London: Routledge.

Zhao, B. (2012). Global trade and Swahili cosmopolitan material culture: Chinese-style ceramic shards from Sanje ya Kati and Songo Mnara (Kilwa, Tanzania). *Journal of World History*, 23 (1), 41–85.

Zhao, B., and Qin, D. (2018). Links with China. In S. Wynne-Jones and A. LaViolette, eds., *The Swahili World*. New York: Routledge, pp. 430–444.

Zhu, T., Ding, X., Kusimba, C. M., and Feng, Z. (2015). Using laser ablation inductively coupled plasma mass spectroscopy (LA-ICP-MS) to determine the provenance of the cobalt pigment of Qinghua porcelain from Jingdezhen in Yuan Dynasty of China (1271–1368 AD). *Ceramics International*, 41 (8), pp. 9878–9884.

Acknowledgments

This Element rests on the theoretical and empirical scholarship of hundreds of researchers and numerous anonymous individuals who are not easy to thank. The references in the sections will acknowledge the intellectual debt I owe to researchers; however, I would be remiss if I failed to acknowledge, at the outset, Richard Davis, George Abungu, Kaingu Kalume, Sibel B. Kusimba, Janet Monge, Mohamed Mchula Mohamed, Gilbert Oteyo, Simiyu Wandibba, Paul Sinclair, and Richard Wilding, whose collaboration in the work on the Swahili coast and inland Kenya has had a great influence on my intellectual and personal development. Geraldine Heng and Susan Noakes's invitation to participate in a workshop on the Global Middle Ages Project in Dar es Salaam in 2012 launched this project. Subsequent seminars at the University of Minnesota in Minneapolis and the University of Texas at Austin allowed me to think about Africa's place in the Global Middle Ages.

My research in Kenya was supported by the National Museums of Kenya and the Republic of Kenya through research permits and excavation permits: 0P/13/001/25C 86; MHE & T 13/001/35C264, NCST/5/C/002/E/543 and NACOSTI/P/17/811175/16914. The bulk of my research in Kenya was carried out when I was a curator of African anthropology at the Field Museum. Bennet Bronson, Bruce Patterson, Charles Stanish, Ed Yastrow, Gary Feinman, James Phillips, James Koepl, James Vanstone, Jonathan Haas, John Terrell, and Scott Lidgard welcomed me each in their own way, and they collectively opened the museum and seamlessly integrated me into a world institution steeped in a rich history of excellence in research. The financial assistance of Misty and Lewis Gruber, Constance Crane, Pierrette Helene Barut, Akiko and Dr. Edward Swabb, Liz and Withrow Meeker, the Women's Board Field Dreams, the Anthropology Alliance, the internship program at the Field Museum, and Ernest and Young sustained a synergy that made Swahili research possible.

Funding through the US National Science Foundation SBR 9024683 (1991–3), BCS 9615291 (1996–8), BCS 0106664 (2002–4), BCS 0352681 (2003–4), BCS 0648762 (2007–9), and BCS-1030081 (2010–12); the US National Endowment for the Humanities (2012–14); the US IIE J. W. Fulbright Sr. Scholars Program (2002–3, 2012); National Geographic Society (1996–7, 2020–1); Wenner–Gren Foundation (1991); and the Royal Anthropological Institute of Great Britain and Ireland (1991) enabled my colleagues and me to develop a regional research program in southeast Kenya that has endured since.

Sibel B. Kusimba has provided dedicated collaboration from the time I planned my first major fieldwork in 1989 to the present. My ideas about the past and how best to unveil it have been shaped by numerous conversations with Akinwumi Ogundiran, Jonathan R. Walz, Charles Stanish, Gary Feinman, Innocent Pikirayi, Joyce Marcus, Peter R. Schmidt, and Vincent Pigott. Rahul C. Oka, Charles Stanish, Sibel B. Kusimba, Geraldine Heng, and Susan Noakes read and offered critical comments on the various drafts of this Element. Janet Monge's meticulous study of the Swahili human remains has enabled us to understand the biological identities and lifestyles of the medieval Swahili peoples. Eric Wert, Foreman Bandama, Gilbert Oteyo, and Jill Seagard drew illustrations in this Element. Marie Georg's careful reading and editing of the Element helped shape its final form. Mathews Wakhungu searched through hundreds of out-of-date CDs and field phones to identify figures for the Element.

I have benefited from the support of the National Museums of Kenya. Simiyu Wandibba, Omar Bwana, Ali Abubakar, George Abungu, Angela Kabiru, and Purity Kiura have cheerfully supported my research efforts. On the coast, Mohamed Mchula, Salim Karisa Mutengo, Kaingu Kalume Tinga, George Gandi, Gilbert Oteyo, and Khalfan Bini Ahmed helped with excavations and analysis of finds at different moments. Paul Mutegi and Mohamed Mchulla Mohamed of Mombasa never stop redefining the concept of true friendship. In Chicago, Ed Yastrow, Bennet Bronson, Bruce Patterson, James Phillips, and Charles Stanish's friendship helped guide a novice isolated from the core Africanist group to launch what has become a truly satisfying life of mind and soul.

In February 2020, I accepted the University of South Florida's offer to join the Institute for the Advanced Study in Culture and the Environment and the Department of Anthropology at the Tampa and St. Petersburg campuses, directed by Professor Charles Stanish who had instigated my hire at the Field Museum nearly three decades earlier. Through the Institute and the anthropology department, I have at my disposal the rare opportunity and resources to develop an exceptional interdisciplinary consortium of scholarship based on current faculty that would immediately have a national and global impact in understanding humankind's place in a rapidly changing universe.

An eight-month lockdown in western Kenya in 2020 gave me the rare opportunity to think about and compose this Element. In these pages, I have returned to the subject that initially drew me into the study of Swahili forty years ago, first as a history major and only later as an anthropological archaeologist. *Swahili Worlds in Globalism* is a culmination of this interdisciplinary odyssey.

Cambridge Elements ☰

The Global Middle Ages

Geraldine Heng

University of Texas at Austin

Geraldine Heng is Perceval Professor of English and Comparative Literature at the University of Texas, Austin. She is the author of *The Invention of Race in the European Middle Ages* (2018) and *England and the Jews: How Religion and Violence Created the First Racial State in the West* (2018), both published by Cambridge University Press, as well as *Empire of Magic: Medieval Romance and the Politics of Cultural Fantasy* (2003, Columbia). She is the editor of *Teaching the Global Middle Ages* (2022, MLA), coedits the University of Pennsylvania Press series, RaceB4Race: Critical Studies of the Premodern, and is working on a new book, *Early Globalisms: The Interconnected World, 500–1500 CE*. Originally from Singapore, Heng is a Fellow of the Medieval Academy of America, a member of the Medievalists of Color, and Founder and Co-director, with Susan Noakes, of the Global Middle Ages Project: www.globalmiddleages.org.

Susan J. Noakes

University of Minnesota–Twin Cities

Susan J. Noakes is Professor of French and Italian at the University of Minnesota – Twin Cities, where she also serves as Chair of the Department of French and Italian. For her many publications in French, Italian, and Comparative Literature, the University In 2009 named her Inaugural Chair in Arts, Design, and Humanities. Her most recent publication is an analysis of Salim Bachi's *L'Exil d'Ovide*, exploring a contemporary writer's reflection on his exile to Europe by comparing it to Ovid's exile to the Black Sea; it appears in Salim Bachi, edited by Agnes Schaffhauser, published in Paris by Harmattan in 2020.

About the Series

Elements in the Global Middle Ages is a series of concise studies that introduce researchers and instructors to an uncentered, interconnected world, c. 500–1500 CE. Individual Elements focus on the globe's geographic zones, its natural and built environments, its cultures, societies, arts, technologies, peoples, ecosystems, and lifeworlds.

Cambridge Elements ☰

The Global Middle Ages

Printed in the United States
by Baker & Taylor Publisher Services